SEARCHING FOR THE SPIRIT OF
AMERICAN DEMOCRACY

Great Barrington Books

Bringing the old and new together in the spirit of W. E. B. Du Bois

∾ An imprint edited by Charles Lemert ∾

Titles Available

Keeping Good Time: Reflections on Knowledge, Power, and People
by Avery F. Gordon (2004)

Going Down for Air: A Memoir in Search of a Subject
by Derek Sayer (2004)

The Souls of Black Folk, 100th Anniversary Edition
by W. E. B. Du Bois, with commentaries by Manning Marable, Charles Lemert, and Cheryl
Townsend Gilkes (2004)

Sociology After the Crisis, Updated Edition
by Charles Lemert (2004)

Subject to Ourselves, by Anthony Elliot (2004)

The Protestant Ethic Turns 100: Essays on the Centenary of the Weber Thesis
edited by William H. Swatos, Jr., and Lutz Kaelber (2005)

Postmodernism Is Not What You Think
by Charles Lemert (2005)

Discourses on Liberation: An Anatomy of Critical Theory
by Kyung-Man Kim (2005)

Seeing Sociologically: The Routine Grounds of Social Action
by Harold Garfinkel, edited and introduced by Anne Warfield Rawls (2005)

The Souls of W. E. B. Du Bois
by Alford A. Young, Jr., Manning Marable, Elizabeth Higginbotham,
Charles Lemert, and Jerry G. Watts (2006)

Radical Nomad: C. Wright Mills and His Times
by Tom Hayden with Contemporary Reflections by Stanley Aronowitz,
Richard Flacks, and Charles Lemert (2006)

Critique for What? Cultural Studies, American Studies, Left Studies
by Joel Pfister (2006)

Social Solutions to Poverty, by Scott Meyers-Lipton (2006)

Everyday Life and the State, by Peter Bratsis (2006)

Thinking the Unthinkable: An Introduction to Social Theories
by Charles Lemert (2007)

Between Citizen and State: An Introduction to the Corporation
by David A. Westbrook (2007)

Politics, Identity, and Emotion, by Paul Hoggett (2009)

Out of Crisis: Rethinking Our Financial Markets, by David A. Westbrook (2010)

Uncertain Worlds: World-Systems Analysis in Changing Times,
by Immanuel Wallerstein, Carlos Aguirre Rojas, and Charles Lemert (2012)

It Ain't Me, Babe: Bob Dylan and the Performance of Authenticity
by Andrea Cossu (2012)

*Searching for the Spirit of American Democracy:
Max Weber's Analysis of a Unique Political Culture, Past, Present, and Future*
by Stephen Kalberg (2014)

Boston
19 February 2015

SEARCHING FOR THE SPIRIT OF AMERICAN DEMOCRACY

Max Weber's Analysis of a Unique
Political Culture, Past, Present, and Future

STEPHEN KALBERG

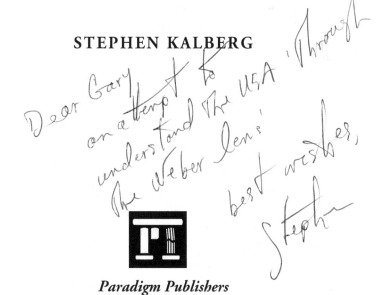

Dear Gary,
on attempt to
understand The USA 'Through
The Weber lens'
best wishes,
Stephen

Paradigm Publishers
Boulder • London

Copyright © 2014 by Paradigm Publishers

Published in the United States by Paradigm Publishers, 5589 Arapahoe Avenue, Boulder, CO 80303 USA.

Paradigm Publishers is the trade name of Birkenkamp & Company, LLC Dean Birkenkamp, President and Publisher.

Library of Congress Cataloging-in-Publication Data

Kalberg, Stephen.
  Searching for the spirit of American democracy : Max Weber's analysis of a unique political culture, past, present, and future / Stephen Kalberg.
      pages cm
  Includes bibliographical references and index.
  ISBN 978-1-61205-444-5 (hardcover : alk. paper)
  ISBN 978-1-61205-430-8 (library e-book)
  ISBN 978-1-61205-445-2 (paperback : alk. paper)
  ISBN 978-1-61205-591-6 (consumer e-book)
  1. Democracy—United States. 2. Political culture—United States.
3. Weber, Max, 1864–1920—Political and social views. I. Title.
  JK1726.K34 2013
  306.20973—dc23

                                                            2013022328

Printed and bound in the United States of America on acid-free paper that meets the standards of the American National Standard for Permanence of Paper for Printed Library Materials.

Typeset by Straight Creek Bookmakers.

18 17 16 15 14   1 2 3 4 5

For Gaya

*[America's] democratic traditions [were] handed down by
Puritanism as an everlasting heirloom.*

—Max Weber, "Capitalism and Rural Society in Germany"

Brief Contents

Acknowledgments   *xii*

Introduction   1

Chapter One   The Foundations I: The Ascetic Protestant
                 Cornerstones of the Early American
                 Political Culture   21

Chapter Two   The Foundations II: The Protestant Sects
                 in the American Colonies, the Early
                 United States, and Beyond   33

Chapter Three   The "Eminent Power" of the American
                 Political Culture to Form Groups:
                 From Sects to Civic Associations,
                 the Civic Sphere, and Practical-Ethical
                 Action in the Nineteenth Century   47

Chapter Four   The Political Culture of the Late
                 Nineteenth and Early Twentieth
                 Centuries: The Strong Individual–
                 Small State Constellation   59

Chapter Five   The Weberian Model: The Dissolution
                 of the American Civic Sphere
                 in the Twentieth Century   68

Chapter Six   Complementary Models: Expanding the
                 Weberian Model   83

Chapter Seven   Conclusion: Max Weber's Analysis
of the Spirit of American Democracy,
Past, Present, and Future   99

Appendix I   The American Journey: Observations and
Ramifications   118

Appendix II   *The Protestant Ethic and the Spirit
of Capitalism*: A Brief Summary   127

Glossary   *136*
Bibliography   *142*
Credits   *151*
Index   *152*
About the Author   *157*

Contents

Acknowledgments   *xii*

Introduction   **1**

    The Political Culture Approach and the
        Spirit of American Democracy   8
    Toward Max Weber: The Past,
        Present, and Future of the American
        Political Culture   10
    The American Political Culture's Central
        Contours and Long-Range Pathways   12
    An Overview   14

Chapter One   **The Foundations I: The Ascetic Protestant
Cornerstones of the Early American
Political Culture**   **21**

    World-Mastery Individualism:
        Religious Origins   22
    Community Activism: Religious Origins   26
        Creating the Kingdom of God   26
        The Ethical Community:
            The Congregation   28

Chapter Two   **The Foundations II: The Protestant Sects
in the American Colonies, the Early
United States, and Beyond**   **33**

    Beyond *The Protestant Ethic*:
        The Protestant Sect   36
    Sect and Church   37

The Sect's Social-Psychological Dynamic:
"Holding Your Own" Individualism,
Conformity, and the Methodical-Rational
Organization of Life   39
The Puritan Sects: Democratic Governance,
Freedom of Conscience, and the
Opposition to Secular Authority   43

**Chapter Three   The "Eminent Power" of the American
Political Culture to Form Groups:
From Sects to Civic Associations,
the Civic Sphere, and Practical-Ethical
Action in the Nineteenth Century**   47
"American Society Is Not a Sandpile"   49
The Expansion of the Congregation's
Values into Communities and the
Formation of a Civic Sphere   51
The Maintenance of Public Ideals and
Civic Ethics: "Practical-Ethical Action"
and the New Symbiotic Dualism   54

**Chapter Four   The Political Culture of the Late
Nineteenth and Early Twentieth Centuries:
The Strong Individual–Small State
Constellation**   59
The View of the State in Industrializing
America   60
Isolating American Uniqueness:
The View of the State in Industrializing
Germany and the Divergent Location
of Practical-Ethical Action   63

**Chapter Five   The Weberian Model: The Dissolution
of the American Civic Sphere in the
Twentieth Century**   68
The Modern World: An Iron Cage?   69
The Weberian Model: The Dissolution
of the Civic Sphere   75
*The Privatization of Work and the Expansion
of Practical Rationalism   75*
*The Circumscription of the Civic Sphere
by "Europeanization"   77*

*The Circumscription of the Civic Sphere
by the "Power of Material Goods" 78*

Chapter Six   **Complementary Models:
Expanding the Weberian Model**   **83**
The Generalization Model: The Civic
Sphere's Longevity 84
*The Role of Moral Values in the 2004
Presidential Election: An Application
of the Generalization Model 85*
The Professional Associations Model:
The Relocation and Narrowing
of the Sect Legacy 88
The Conflict Model: The Contested
Civic Sphere 91

Chapter Seven **Conclusion: Max Weber's Analysis
of the Spirit of American Democracy,
Past, Present, and Future**   **99**
Reviewing the Argument 102
*A Colonial Era Symbiotic Dualism 102
The Nineteenth Century: A Civic-Oriented
Individualism and a New Symbiotic
Dualism 103*
Lessons from the Unusual American Case? 106
The Weberian Mode of Analysis: Studying
Political Cultures 109

Appendix I   **The American Journey: Observations and
Ramifications**   **118**

Appendix II   ***The Protestant Ethic and the Spirit
of Capitalism*: A Brief Summary**   **127**

Glossary   *136*
Bibliography   *142*
Credits   *151*
Index   *152*
About the Author   *157*

Acknowledgments

PERHAPS THE IDEAS in this volume were manifest earliest in my article "Tocqueville and Weber" (1997). Over the years, and largely owing to discussions with students in my Political Culture seminar at Boston University, a number of themes began to crystallize more clearly. I would particularly like to thank my students Maryam Arif, Christopher Byrnes, Zophia Edwards, Michael Ferron, Priyanka Kotadis, Yuichi Moroi, Stephanie Mott, Tereza Novotna, Lauren Olofson, Samantha Ricks, and Theresa Strachila for their thoughtful comments.

Several colleagues have raised difficult questions that forced me repeatedly to undertake revisions of central chapters. Their suggestions have improved this study far beyond what it otherwise would have been. I am deeply indebted to Robert J. Antonio, James R. Kent, Charles Lemert, Donald Nielsen, Guenther Roth, and Lawrence A. Scaff.

Finally, it is difficult to imagine that this book could have assumed its present contours had I not lived abroad for many years. It has benefited from innumerable discussions with European friends on the nature of American society. They bestowed upon me both "distance and nearness" to the American political culture.

Introduction

DESPITE STRONG DISAGREEMENT along a series of axes, an overarching dividing line marked the American presidential campaign of 2012. The self-reliance maxim—"I can make it on my own"—stood in stark contrast to another familiar adage: "We are all in this together, and we must create a sharing national community." Both Governor Romney's plea for small government and strong individuals and President Obama's call for a spirit of compassion resounded widely. Although seemingly contradictory, both poles of this self-reliance/shared-community spectrum constitute core components of the American *spirit of democracy*. Moreover, they extend far into this nation's past.

Both sides have been apparent since John Winthrop's tenure as governor of Massachusetts in the seventeenth century. We must "labor together" for the "common good," he proclaimed, in order to create the "shining city on the hill" that demonstrates God's majesty. However, as individuals alone before God, we are directly responsible for our own beliefs and our own destiny.

Likewise, this spectrum was highly visible when the Founders aligned themselves into Jeffersonians and Hamiltonians and, as well, in the nineteenth century. Now "heroic individuals" pulled themselves up "by their bootstraps" and "rugged individuals" conquered the frontier. Other Americans assisted newly arrived immigrants and founded volunteer organizations in order to "give back" to their communities. "Public service" and philanthropic activity became widespread.

These two poles also reverberated throughout the twentieth century. Indeed, the orientations of Americans to private interests *and* civic

1

improvement endured in spite of a great transformation: a youthful nation populated largely by small farmers became a nation of urban dwellers engaged in highly specialized tasks performed in factories and offices. The resilience of the self-reliance/shared-community spectrum appears remarkable. A visitor from the eighteenth century would recognize today's political landscape.

It still encompasses these ideals. The "can-do" attitudes of persons on a quest for self-reliance stand alongside of, and occasionally merge with, a commitment by individuals to the well-being of their communities. Americans are "self-made," independent, and capable of choosing—and then pursuing—"individual opportunity" and an upwardly mobile path. Many believe that "government action" is only rarely legitimate. However, we also feel obligated to each other and prepared to contribute to our nation's *civic* life, as Martin Luther King and John F. Kennedy called upon all Americans to do.[1] Owing to a "common bond" and a "shared destiny," public service on behalf of civic betterment is expected. We volunteer far more frequently than do citizens of other nations, and we speak of a "dedication" to improve our communities. We hope for a "compassionate nation." Individualism is praised, yet excessive individualism is condemned in just these terms—namely, as lacking "selfless engagement" and a civic element.[2]

Despite their endurance and concerted impact throughout our history, these two poles of the American political spectrum have at times fallen into a relationship of antagonism. The high decibel level apparent throughout the electoral campaign of 2012 offered clear evidence of this decoupling. Now appropriated by a major political party, each pole seems to unfold along its own trajectory.

The 2012 election exposed the fault lines just below the surface. They stubbornly endure—and have once again become pronounced. Direct questions appear unavoidable: Does this splintering constitute yet another manifestation of a normal oscillation across the familiar spectrum, albeit one exacerbated by an election campaign's rhetoric? Or have this nation's lines of division now introduced in overt forms a genuine disruption of the three-hundred-year pendulum motion? Has the internal compass bestowed upon American society by the self-reliance/shared-community spectrum lost its hold? Is the American political landscape in a state of severe crisis?

Innumerable recent observers have discovered deep fragmentation and a loss of community life. Falling participation rates have been documented in arrays of organizations, from labor unions to Rotary clubs and parent-teacher associations. Diminished engagement in groups, the commentators contend, decreases—owing to isolation—individuals' influence upon the political arena, whether at the local, state, or federal levels. Even "strong individuals" increasingly experience a sense of powerlessness.

A new mode of decision making has crystallized, these analysts argue, one that threatens the American spirit of democracy: personal interests have come to the forefront as participation in civic activities has declined. To the same extent, a deterioration of community cohesion and a general privatization of life has followed, many observers contend. The idea of an *obligation* to serve one's community resonates less and less. "Community projects" have been frequently unveiled as serving private interests and devoid of a civic element; reference to our "shared destiny" often seems disingenuous.

Robert Putnam's metaphor—Americans are more and more "bowling alone" (2000)—captures well this civic sphere contraction. In order to inhibit or even curtail this trend, many propose an intensification of various socialization mechanisms, following the French founder of modern sociology, Emile Durkheim. They also seek a strengthening of civic associations, following Durkheim and Alexis de Tocqueville. Can a rejuvenation of the American spirit of democracy occur in this manner?[3]

In very recent years, this "American crisis" discussion has acquired new contributors and an altered line of emphasis. The "new crisis" commentators also argue that a vibrant civic realm remains indispensable. However, it will not arise wherever power and wealth remain concentrated in the hands of small elites, they hold, as is increasingly the case in the United States. Many maintain that a wide distribution of political power and economic wealth constitutes a social precondition for the existence of a middle class oriented beyond immediate economic interests and toward participation and service. This deeper dysfunction in American society is not addressed, they insist, by an intensification of socialization mechanisms and a strengthening of civic associations.

These observers see a significant diminution of the middle class in the years following the 2008 collapse of the economy. Moreover, amid a stark polarization of income levels and a heretofore unimagined concentration of wealth and power among a minute few, the middle class has proven less and less able to resist a deleterious development: a harsh colonization of the civic sphere by wealthy political and economic elites. A new plutocracy now reigns, the new crisis analysts argue, and the interests of a tiny segment of the population are now dominant. A "New Gilded Age," characterized now by a crass manipulation of public opinion by hegemonic powers, is on the horizon, they warn.[4]

To these commentators, under these circumstances a shared community and viable civic sphere appear utopian. A society now exists in which the interests of the powerful reign, they contend. Will minimal upward mobility and severe inequality become widely accepted? If this new "radical inequality" prevails, the American Dream and community-sharing ideals will gradually dissipate and fade, as will the self-reliance ethos, the new crisis observers maintain.

Many prominent commentators across the political horizon insist that a crucial turning point now confronts the United States. They view this nation as entering a critical epoch, one characterized by a loss of continuity with the past, a weakening of civic life, and inequalities of unusual severity. Some observers hold that a new trajectory has already been charted, one in which the strength of the once-vibrant civic sphere continues to be sapped and "social atomism" expands. Indeed, alarms from various corners over the last fifteen years have regularly proclaimed the "severe dysfunction" of the American political landscape.

The deterioration of *both poles* of this spirit of democracy spectrum implies new, and uncharted, transformations. A period of troubled questioning has commenced, all analysts argue. Perhaps it will be marked by a complete disappearance of the pendulum oscillations typical of this spirit. And new configurations will remain powerless to nourish the functioning civic sphere indispensable to a democratic mode of governance, they contend. Privatized interests and goals will exclusively infuse individualism. These worries and concerns bear directly upon this volume's query: Does an American spirit of democracy still exist that is capable of lending strong legitimacy and support to a stable, open, and functioning democracy?

Although pitched debates on these urgent issues abound today, investigations on the origins and development of the components at the foundation of the American spirit of democracy are scarcely to be found. What were its early features? How did they arise and expand? How did they nourish the practice of self-governance? What sources played a role? Do the same sources *endure* even today? If so, to what degree do they exhibit a clear influence? The present-day discussions omit a great deal.

Scrutiny of the American spirit of democracy's deep cultural elements and long historical roots must be brought into this broad national discussion. Embedded and firm, its centuries-old axes have endured, often in secular forms, into the present—despite large-scale social, political, and economic change. Many historians insist that great continuities over centuries are evident. The crisis authors, they maintain, focus their analyses too narrowly upon recent developments and attempt to comprehend the present while neglecting its deep entanglement with the past.

For their part, the crisis commentators continue to point to immediate and injurious transformations. They hold their ground—and the debate continues. Again, does the American spirit of democracy *still* provide adequate legitimacy and sustenance to the operating mechanisms of an open and stable American democracy? Or are this spirit's long-standing parameters and patterned oscillations undergoing a severe metamorphosis and turning now in new—and dysfunctional—directions?

Opponents of the new crisis authors articulate a further theme: They maintain that these analysts omit rigorous and systematic procedures. Too often their descriptions of the present rely upon unrepresentative cases and even anecdotal examples, they argue. As importantly, in interpreting the present, the crisis commentators fail to offer standardized and clearly defined concepts, their critics insist.

On behalf of a more accurate understanding of the American spirit of democracy *today*, this volume addresses this ongoing debate. It attempts to do so by using rigorous concepts and procedures—that is, a clear mode of analysis.

This study also seeks to describe the present-day contours of the American *political culture* within which this spirit of democracy is embedded. However, it does so in a manner quite at variance from the new crisis authors. Rather than focusing on features of this political culture today (its new inequality and concentration of political and economic power, for example), it takes a historical turn—ultimately to the era of America's founding: the seventeenth and eighteenth centuries. The *deep historical* roots of today's political culture and, in particular, of the two poles of its spirit of democracy, become our theme at the outset (Chapters 1 and 2). Nevertheless, far from dwelling on America's distant past, this volume moves quickly to a major task: to define, in these chapters and in succinct form, the *track* along which the American political culture developed. Having done so, we turn to a further main goal: to assess the impact of the early American political culture upon later centuries. Its major streams, it is here assumed, left powerful legacies. A few filtrated significantly into our own era.

These legacies are then explored. Their contours are demarcated and their influence in the nineteenth and twentieth centuries is evaluated. Indeed, the early American spirit of democracy, it will be argued, proved capable of *guiding* in this later era the American political culture's development. And even today it does so to a significant extent, Chapters 5 and 6 maintain—even to an important degree serving to sustain the present-day operational workings of American self-governance. Comprehension of the spirit of American democracy's historical development *to the present* is indispensable, this volume holds, for an adequate understanding of its impact upon the American political landscape today. Awareness of this long-range trajectory sheds a crucial beam of light that assists our understanding of the American political landscape at its present state of development.

At this point, this investigation clashes directly with the general focus of the crisis commentators upon the present. It conflicts as well with their neglect of the American political culture.

Thus, this study, addressing throughout the American political culture, attempts to bring a *historical dimension* into ongoing debates. While abjuring the "strong continuity" position taken by some historians today, it nonetheless contends that the new crisis authors' predominant focus on the present omits too much. In particular, this stance precludes recognition of a pivotal and deeply rooted aspect of the American political landscape today: its political culture. Legacies of the Colonial era's political culture were rejuvenated by a series of developments in the nineteenth century (see Chapters 3 and 4) and pushed forward, as a spirit of democracy, indeed even into the twentieth and twenty-first centuries, it is argued. Their influence, albeit weakened and often concealed below the surface, remained—and these legacies must not be neglected. A nation's political culture unavoidably *links* the past with the present.

Furthermore, *whether* the American political culture is experiencing severe and transformational alterations today must be evaluated in reference to a palette of causal factors far broader than those discussed by the new crisis commentary. The historical dimension must be included in the ongoing debate not only because it casts light upon the quandaries and dilemmas confronting the American political landscape today, but also because doing so extends the range of causal factors under consideration. Only such a qualitative expansion will allow an adequate assessment of the severity of present-day dilemmas.

Fulfillment of this complex task requires powerful assistance. This study seeks guidance throughout from sociology's preeminent theorist of deep culture and past-present linkages: Max Weber. His definition of political cultures also proves useful here: for him, because they are constituted from arrays of cohesive and long-standing beliefs and values, political cultures strongly link the past to the present.

However, this study turns to this classical theorist for assistance in a further manner: his sociology offers guidance in regard to the selection of appropriate concepts and procedures.[5] Indeed, his rigorous *mode of analysis* rooted in "ideal types" provides crucial assistance throughout this study. As will become apparent, his concepts and procedures contribute a systematic element to this investigation that is lacking in the works of the new crisis commentators.

In sum, this study seeks to offer insight and understanding regarding the contours and parameters of the American political landscape today. Its rejection at the outset of the predominant orientation to the present and the constricted inventory of causal forces articulated by the new crisis commentators directs our analysis down a complex, long historical pathway. Hence, this investigation's ambitions are high: it aims to *combine* a clear and precise demarcation of the American *political culture today* with full cognizance of the many ways in which even the distant past—in the form of a distinct spirit of democracy—enters into and influences the present. One of this volume's major tasks is to explain how this has occurred.

This dual orientation to the past and the present distinguishes this study clearly from those offered by the new crisis analysts. Moreover, the forceful acknowledgment here of the many ways in which the past penetrates deeply into the present places into a broad contextual tapestry the "self-reliant" and "shared community" poles manifest *alike* in the long-standing American spirit of democracy and the 2012 presidential campaign. The deep roots of each of these poles—and the major causes behind their staying power—will be examined in this investigation. In addition, the ways in which they have endured over centuries in a *symbiotic* relationship will be traced out in considerable detail. Neglected by present-day commentators, the profound *interaction* of the self-reliant and shared community poles also distinguishes the American spirit of democracy.

Two tasks must be addressed before commencing explorations in these directions. A definition at the outset of the political culture approach at the foundation of this volume proves indispensable. We must then examine the ways in which Max Weber's analysis of the American political culture can assist clarification generally as well as attainment of our goals to offer greater understanding *and* at least partial causal explanations. Using Weber will especially unveil the original American political culture's constitutive values and their nineteenth-century manifestations, trajectory, and impact. We seek then to assess whether, sustained by this political culture, a spirit of American democracy remained influential in the twentieth century. If still forceful, is its impact significant today (Chapter 7)? We first turn to the task of defining a nation's political culture.

The Political Culture Approach and the Spirit of American Democracy

The political culture perspective attempts to define, and render overt, the beliefs and values that undergird the daily conduct of politics. What beliefs and values underlie policy making? They account for a particular posture—or ethos—of citizens, it is here maintained, in respect to their political views, degree of civic participation, and habitus in regard to authority, equality, the competition of pluralistic groups, and self-governance in general. Moreover, scholars oriented to political cultures stress the uniqueness of each nation's values-based infrastructure and attempt to comprehend its formation as a long-term, largely indigenous process. Salient to them are *both* the centuries-old historical roots of the present value configuration *and* the extent to which today's values facilitate—or hinder—the growth and stability of representative democracy.

Most proponents of the political culture approach insist that the capacity of citizens to initiate and sustain a *civic sphere* is fundamental to a democratic political culture. This bounded arena located "between" the state and the solitary individual "pulls" citizens beyond privatized, interest-based, and utilitarian concerns into a realm in which *common values* constitute strong ideals. Furthermore, on the basis of its values, the civic sphere defends free participation, the expression of individual rights, and the open competition of groups, it is argued. Lastly, it legitimizes a broad and diverse spectrum of explicitly political activities.

Hence, on the one hand the *birth and growth* of a viable civic sphere remains a clear focus of research. Here the *capacity* of this arena to orient the activity of persons and to assist the growth of civic associations and representative democracy is central. On the other hand the *weakening* of this sphere in the twenty-first century—and the myriad consequences that follow—becomes a central line of investigation.

Major questions relevant to students of political cultures can now be formulated in a concrete and familiar manner. For example,

> For what reasons do civic associations independent from the state arise, expand, and become viewed as legitimate?
>
> How do they sustain their independence over longer time frames?
>
> What are major features of the social contexts that allow, and even support, various forms of citizen participation, including engagement in civic-sphere groups?
>
> How do innumerable and competing groups arise in certain social contexts to such an extent that hegemony is denied to a single cohesive group?
>
> Under what circumstances does respect for the state's authority assume an exaggerated form that threatens the civic sphere's independence?

Eight overarching questions guide this exploration of the *American* political culture. What constellations of values and beliefs—or "spirit"—stood at its foundation? What were its sources? In what ways have the birth and longevity of American democracy been influenced by the contours of its spirit of democracy? Have its major elements now, in the second decade of the twenty-first century, changed? If so, do its new components also serve to lend values-based support to representative democracy? Do Americans continue to cultivate a spirit of democracy? If so, does a self-reliance and "can-do" ethos remain in a symbiotic relationship with a "community-building" set of values? Or have these two poles separated today, as the 2012 presidential campaign seems to indicate?

These queries endow this volume with a clear direction. It seeks to discover, demarcate, and explain the origins of the values and beliefs— the spirit of democracy—at the foundation of the American political culture, to trace the influence of this spirit, and to evaluate whether a present-day political culture supports or opposes the functioning of representative democracy in the United States today.

This study pursues this agenda at the outset by placing the longer-term and overarching values and beliefs of the American political culture at center stage. However, if lacking a clear theoretical framework, all systematic rigor will elude this far-ranging project. Wide-scale guidance is necessary—and thus guidance has been sought from sociology's greatest theorist of deep culture and the multidimensional impact of the past upon the present.

Toward Max Weber: The Past, Present, and Future of the American Political Culture

The American political culture's fault lines introduce many puzzles and dilemmas. Delineation of the distinct sources, particular parameters, unique trajectories, and singular impact of its spirit of democracy presents a large task. Weber's complex mode of analysis proves capable of capturing this spirit.[6] It does so by framing pivotal questions and defining the American political culture's origins, contours, pathways, and influence.

This investigation first focuses on the long historical roots and specific features of the political culture that underpins American self-governance. In seeking to define its distinct origins and impact through a Weberian lens, this study explores the spirit of democracy that assisted at this nation's birth and then helped to sustain the American form of representative government. In particular, this volume examines the American Colonies and the United States from the vantage point of the values and beliefs surrounding the birth of its civic sphere and the further values and beliefs that facilitated its resilience and endurance.[7] Chapters 6 and 7 evaluate whether this nation's spirit of democracy *today* continues to support American democracy's stable functioning.

Weber's works offer concepts and procedures that serve these goals. Their orientation to long-range causes assists understanding of the profound ways in which values and beliefs embedded in the Colonial era's political culture anchored essential features of the American civic sphere in the nineteenth century—and even today. Furthermore, his mode of analysis supports our aim to define, and to explain causally, the *unique* origins, value content, pathways, and impact of the American spirit of democracy.

These aspects of Weber's sociology throw many basic tenets held by opposing schools into sharp relief. He insists that capitalism's advance, "modernization processes" in general, and the "rational choices" of individuals fail to explain adequately the sources, singularity, trajectory, and impact of the American political culture. And reference to a massive expansion of the economy, the political and economic interests of powerful classes, and the interests of privileged groups will not alone provide satisfactory explanations, according to Weber. Moreover, because they are too global and imprecise, macrostructural transformations—from tradition to modernity, particularism to universalism, rural economies to urban economies, and feudalism to capitalism and modern democracy—never articulate the unique features of a *specific* nation's political culture and historical pathway, he contends. Weber's attention to the embedding of the present in the past, and to the ways in which value configurations *may* shape even the interests behind political and economic developments, consistently opposes all diffuse, monocausal, and surface-level approaches.

Was the longevity of this nation's democracy, and its comparative stability, even amid civil war and a metamorphosis from an agrarian to a modern capitalist economy, in part a consequence of a political culture supportive of a spirit of democracy? To Weber, reference to the Constitution's checks and balances mechanism and the "wisdom" and "rational choices" of American citizens must be perceived as offering helpful, but inadequate, modes of explanation.

More complex concepts and procedures—a *Weberian* approach—prove indispensable, this volume argues, for an understanding of the sources, original values, endurance, and impact of the American spirit of democracy. Investigation along these lines will allow an evaluation, in Chapters 2 through 6, of this political culture's *influence* on the 220-year duration of American democracy.

Chapter 1 formulates many of this volume's major arguments. Unlike the sketches and impressions of innumerable early commentators upon "American life," Weber perpetually *framed* his observations. Indeed, they developed into a systematic analysis—one that linked the present with the past, exhibited a consistent terminology, identified multitudes of interrelationships and causal flows, and articulated an empirically based mode of analysis. His approach attains a degree of rigor only rarely achieved by interpreters of American society.

This study's overriding themes must be explored in more precise form. A brief introduction to the American political culture will serve this purpose. Characteristics perceived by Weber as integral to its spirit of democracy are discussed in the following section; key dimensions are laid out. An overview of each chapter then follows. The contribution of each to this study's major concepts, orientations, themes, and goals will be summarized.

The American Political Culture's Central Contours and Long-Range Pathways

Weber discovers overarching continuities in American history and often locates their sources in the religion arena. "The modern person," he contends, "seems generally unable to imagine *how* large a significance those components of our consciousness rooted in religious beliefs have actually had upon culture and ... the organization of life" (2011c, p. 178).

Scarcely visible to us today, seventeenth- and eighteenth-century religious values laid down *the tracks* within which the American political culture would develop, he insists.[8] Its foundational features were defined by an enormous task to be undertaken by ascetic Protestants, or Puritans:[9] to establish God's equitable and just kingdom on earth. These disciplined believers[10] constructed an unusual *symbiotic dualism*:[11] a "world-mastery" (*Weltbeherrschung*) individualism oriented to initiative-taking, and a vigorous overcoming of obstacles became conjoined with the aim to erect cohesive communities organized strictly around a demanding God's ethical standards.[12]

Weber's analysis of the ways in which a pragmatic mode of ethical action—*practical-ethical* individualism[13]—arose in the nineteenth century out of Puritan legacies proves pivotal. The direct pathway from the early goal to create God's kingdom on earth to the appearance in this century of multitudes of secular civic associations remains central. He calls attention to the unusual capacity of these cohesive groups to introduce quasi-religious values broadly into public life. Over many generations these values became endowed with a sustaining thrust, one that endured despite the massive social transformations that accompanied industrialization and urbanization. A civic *sphere* crystallized, indeed to such a degree that it proved capable of uprooting even "strong and self-reliant" American individuals *from* privatized interests. Reference to such long-range developments allows comprehension, Weber stresses, of religion's expansive impact on the values indigenous to the American political culture—and thus on a cornerstone component of American democracy.

His analysis emphasizes in this manner a *new* symbiotic dualism, one constituted in the nineteenth century from a practical-ethical individualism on the one hand and a viable orientation of action to a civic sphere on the other hand. Indebted to its Puritan counterpart in the seventeenth and eighteenth centuries, these mutually affirming components must be comprehended as specific to the American spirit of democracy, Weber maintains.

Moreover, they contributed to the longevity of democracy in the United States, he argues. He placed special stress on the alteration of the "social carriers" of values and beliefs that took place in the nineteenth century—namely, from sects and churches to civic associations.[14] These groups, grounded also in a community-building ethos and parallel in internal structure to the Puritan sects, systematically confronted and held in check activity oriented exclusively toward pragmatic, a-ethical calculations. Rather than seeking to construct explicitly a Kingdom of God in strict conformity with His commandments, members of these associations sought to alter communities on behalf of secular *ethical standards and principles.*

However, in the twentieth century a severe weakening and dislocation of these civic associations occurred, Weber contends. This development will strike the American spirit of democracy at its core, he holds: practical-ethical individualism, as cultivated in civic associations, now loses its internal energy. As industrialization and urbanization proceeded, a *practical-rational* individualism replaced this *civic-oriented* individualism in the twentieth century, Weber insists. As this occurred, utilitarian activity more and more effectively contested practical-ethical action and expanded. He queries whether American society will be characterized by impersonal and cold relationships devoid of compassion. Will it approximate an "iron cage"?

Chapters 1 through 6 reconstruct this winding pathway from seventeenth-century Puritans seeking to fulfill God's Will to the twentieth century's widespread practical-rational individualism. The underlying, deep culture elements of American policy making and politics in general—a *political culture* anchored in a singular *spirit of democracy* and its transformations in the twentieth and twenty-first centuries—remain our concern throughout.

An Overview

Chapter 1 addresses the "world-mastery" individualism of the early Puritans in New England and their goal to create on earth a divine ethical community. To Weber, the American political culture's original symbiotic dualism and foundational tracks, as noted, are evident in the seventeenth and eighteenth centuries.

We then examine ascetic Protestantism's carrier groups: religious *sects.* Chapter 2 explores how, in these organizations, a social-psychological, symbiotic dualism gave rise to unusual patterns of action *and* a rare configuration: a "hold your own" individualism directed to ethical standards and community goals, an intense social conformism, and a disciplined—an ascetic—organization of the believer's life. This constellation sustained major aspects of Puritanism's world-mastery individualism throughout the eighteenth century. The sects also placed into motion a strong skepticism regarding all secular authority and tutored the devout on a continuous basis in the art of self-governance. They extended Puritan beliefs far beyond New England. Some gave birth to a notion of freedom of conscience.

Chapter 3 turns to the secularized carriers in the nineteenth century of central Puritan values and modes of action: civic associations. The wide expansion of these groups across the American landscape led Weber to reject the predominant view of the United States among his German colleagues: American society is best characterized as a "sandpile" of unconnected individuals. His analysis of the Puritan origins of the practical-ethical individualism nourished in these associations is summarized, as is his discussion of their unusually effective community-building capacities. They introduced, as noted, a new symbiotic dualism.

Chapter 4 investigates the "strong individual–small state" constellation unique to the American political culture of the late nineteenth and early twentieth centuries. Its religious sources, as located in the seventeenth and eighteenth centuries, are outlined. This configuration is then contrasted with major features of Germany's political culture of the late nineteenth century. The precise contours and uniqueness of the American symbiotic dualism become evident through this comparative case. As well, legacies of Puritanism's world-mastery and community-building vigor become apparent in this chapter.

Chapter 5 first summarizes briefly Weber's analysis of the origins, expansion, and manifestations of a crucial component in the American spirit of democracy: its civic sphere. It then addresses whether the significant transformations indicate an approximation of the American political culture to Weber's famous "iron cage" metaphor. Has its spirit of democracy vanished? Can it accurately be characterized as a "steel-hard casing"?[15] Does this image, which evokes a closed and bureaucratized society devoid of relationships of compassion, facilitate understanding of this political culture? After an exploration of its common usage, Weber's exact definition is reconstructed and the Weberian model is formulated.

The latter section of Chapter 5 turns to the twentieth and twenty-first centuries and formulates a *Weberian model*. This construct indicates a circumscription and weakening of the civic sphere owing to the "privatization of work," "Europeanization," and the "increasing power of material goods." An expansion of practical rationalism follows as does a disappearance of this nation's spirit of democracy. To what extent, we query, does this model accurately capture major features of the contemporary American political culture? Does it conform to a great degree to the political culture described by the new crisis commentators today?

Using further concepts and procedures borrowed directly from Weber, Chapter 6 erects an alternative model. The three sub-constructs of this *Complementary model* conceptualize differently the complex parameters of the American political culture today. The "Generalization" sub-construct postulates that legacies of civic individualism remain vigorous and formidable influences to this day. Moreover, they interlock, in this sub-model, with a *viable* civic sphere—indeed, to such a degree that the nineteenth century's symbiotic dualism endures. This spirit of American democracy dualism again serves to periodically reinvigorate practical-ethical action, civic associations, and a civic sphere. All thrusts toward a circumscription of the civic sphere by bureaucratization, the power of material goods, and the privatization of work are held effectively in check as a consequence of this rejuvenated spirit of democracy. Does this model accurately depict the American political culture of today?

This sub-construct constitutes only one possible alternative to the Weberian model. Chapter 6 then extends Weberian concepts and procedures in a manner that leads to the formation of two additional sub-models. With the "Professional associations" sub-construct, the legacies of Puritan asceticism and civic individualism remain influential. However, they become *located narrowly*—namely, exclusively in these organizations. Here the civic sphere loses its values-based, ethical core and becomes debilitated as a consequence of practical rationalism's

unchecked aggrandizement. Does this model more adequately conceptualize American society's political culture today?

This chapter's "Conflict" model captures yet a further possibility.
Here legacies of practical-ethical action oriented to a viable civic sphere
survive. However, this civic individualism, owing to its appearance in
weakened forms, fails to subdue practical rationalism. Antagonism is
open and tensions perpetual.

In this manner, Chapters 5 and 6 formulate *Weberian* and *Complementary* models. As noted, each implies three sub-constructs. Taken
together, all sub-models demarcate a twentieth- and twenty-first-
century *American spectrum*. Its parameters, it is argued, delimit this
nation's spirit of democracy of the *present and near-term future*. This
analysis views the political arena's significant developments today as
occurring along this spectrum.

The Conclusion (Chapter 7) first offers a summary of Weber's analysis. The symbiotic dualisms of both the Colonial and nineteenth-century
eras are reviewed and compared; their uniqueness is emphasized. Central
questions are then formulated: Can *lessons* be learned from this charting
out of the complex spirit of democracy at the foundation of the American political culture and its enduring mode of self-governance? Does
the origin and development of *this* political culture provide guidelines
to social scientists and political leaders near and far in search of both
a spirit of democracy and a stable representative democracy? Or does
the "exceptional" character of the American political culture preclude
its transference to other nations or regions? The orientation in Weber's
methodology to cases and the "historical individual" is stressed.

These queries lead our investigation once again back to Weber's *mode
of analysis*. Its boundaries vis-à-vis other schools are again defined and
its several arguments against a widely held view—the formulation of
laws should be the aim of the social sciences—are examined. Just in
this respect several basic tenets of Weber's sociology are emphasized:
the centrality of ideal types, the opposition to organic holism, the
multicausal methodology, and the rejection of "single road maps."

We then turn to various considerations relevant to this volume's
focus on the ways in which political cultures, as constituted from certain long-standing sets of beliefs and values, *may* sustain representative

democracy. We investigate whether supportive political cultures can be viewed as causally significant for the birth and longevity of such a mode of governance. Finally, from the vantage point of Weber's rigorous and long-term analysis, we revisit today's crisis. Weaknesses in the "crisis commentary" can now be defined more clearly.

Two appendices close this volume. The first, by offering a brief account of Weber's sojourn in the United States in 1904, summarizes his perceptions of a political culture fundamentally different from that of his native Germany. This journey influenced his thinking in significant ways. Perhaps the "outsider's perspective" stood at the foundation of his many insights. Appendix II summarizes Weber's famous "Protestant ethic thesis." It examines central technical aspects of his argument left unexplored, although pivotal, in Chapters 1 through 4. A review of this section is recommended to the reader unfamiliar with this thesis. A glossary follows the appendices.

Notes

1. "Ask *not* what your country can do for you; ask what *you* can do for your country" (inaugural address, January 1960).

2. Most of the terms in this paragraph can be found in President Obama's campaign speeches, as well as in his victory speech on November 7, 2012.

3. Several hundred books have been written on these themes by journalists and scholars. Distinguished volumes by "Communitarians" of the 1990s and 2000s include those by Putnam 2000; Etzioni 1997, 1998; Etzioni, Volmert, and Rothschild 2004; and Selznick 1992, 2004. Nearly all of these studies were influenced by Robert Bellah et al., *Habits of the Heart* (1985; see also Bellah 1992). In turn, this volume (as the Communitarian literature generally) owed a strong debt to Tocqueville's *Democracy in America* (1945 [1835]) and Durkheim's *Division of Labor in Society* (1984 [1893]) and *Suicide* (1951 [1897]).

4. These themes are likewise discussed by innumerable authors. Perhaps most influential have been works by Reich 2008, 2011, 2012; Wolin 2008; Klein 2007, 2010; Judt 2011; Barlett and Steele 2012; Hacker and Pierson 2010; Stiglitz 2012; Dobbs 2006; Carville and Greenberg 2012; Faux 2012; Luce 2012; and Nussbaum 2010. These authors, many of whom respond directly to the Communitarians, trace their lineage most clearly back to the

neo-Marxism of Critical Theory (in particular to Habermas [1962]); see also Arato and Gebhardt 1982; Bronner and Kellner 1989; and Kellner 1989. Ultimately, it runs in the United States back to John Dewey (1922, 1989), who described a weakened civic sphere nearly one century ago, and to Thorstein Veblen (1953).

5. The phrases "concepts and procedures" and "mode of analysis" will be used synonymously. Occasionally, "Weber's methodology" will be used.

6. All major attempts to define this nation's political culture have been surrounded by enduring controversy. See, for example, the extensive debates that accompanied the receptions of Riesman, *The Lonely Crowd* (1961); Almond and Verba, *The Civic Culture* (1963); Bellah et al., *Habits of the Heart* (1985); and Putnam, *Bowling Alone* (2000).

7. Praise for, or critique of, the American political culture lies far removed from the goals of this study.

8. I am basing this statement on Weber's famous passage: "Not ideas, but material and ideal interests, directly govern a person's activity. Yet very frequently, the 'world views' that have been created by 'ideas' have, like switchmen, determined the tracks along which action has been pushed by the dynamic of interest. 'From what' and 'for what' one wished to be 'saved' and, let us not forget, could be saved, depended upon one's world view" (2009, p. 241). The American "tracks," in this study, are defined in Chapters 1 and 2.

9. Following Weber, this term refers to the Calvinist (Presbyterian), Methodist, Baptist, Mennonite, and Quaker churches and sects (see 2011c, pp. 158–179). "Puritanism" and "ascetic Protestantism" are used synonymously.

10. The adjectives *disciplined, initiative-taking, activist, strong, stalwart,* and *self-reliant* are here employed basically synonymously. A positive evaluation is not implied. Rather, all seek to convey a focused, energetic, and directed individualism empowered to address and surmount obstacles. It is capable of *organizing* activity in a *patterned* and systematic way. An element of *asceticism* is implied. See Chapter 2.

11. The author has introduced this expression. It remains central throughout the entire discussion of Weber's analysis offered in this volume. See Glossary.

12. Appendix II offers a summary of the major aspects of Weber's complex "Protestant ethic thesis."

13. This is Weber's term. It is defined in more detail immediately below. See also the Glossary.

14. "Social carriers" should be noted at the outset as a concept central throughout this volume. See the Glossary.

15. "Iron cage" and "steel-hard casing" will be employed here synonymously. The former, stemming from the translation by Talcott Parsons of

The Protestant Ethic and the Spirit of Capitalism (Weber 1930), can scarcely be avoided owing to its institutionalization in the social sciences. "Steel-hard casing" constitutes a more accurate rendering of *stahlhartes Gehäuse*. The issues involved are discussed by the author in some detail elsewhere (see Weber 2011c, pp. 397–398, n. 133 [translator's note]). See also the Glossary.

CHAPTER ONE

The Foundations I

The Ascetic Protestant Cornerstones
of the Early American Political Culture

> The autonomy of the individual [in the sect] is anchored not to passivity, but to religious positions, and the struggle against all types of "authoritarian" arbitrariness is here elevated to the level of a religious duty. In the time of its heroic youth [in the sects], this individualism produced an eminent power to form groups.
>
> —*Weber 2011a, pp. 230–231*

THIS CHAPTER EXPLORES the ways in which ascetic Protestantism in the seventeenth and eighteenth centuries gave birth to and sustained the American political culture. Weber maintains that it cultivated a practical-ethical, world-mastery individualism in two demarcated realms: work and community engagement. Thus, *religion* anchored pivotal components of American society, he insists. Remarkably, as will become clear in Chapter 3, this same source proved instrumental in calling forth a secular civic sphere in the nineteenth century.

A fundamental belief in the capacity of persons to influence political processes seems indispensable if a civic sphere is to become salient. Traditions, whether in the form of customs, conventions, values, or social hierarchies, are no longer perceived as enveloping and rigid. Resignation, severe caution, and an inability to take initiative—fatalism in general—no longer reign. However, a capacity to influence political processes and a civic sphere never develop of their own accord, Weber contends, as the political and economy realms—a "public" sphere—expand with urbanization and industrialization.

Instead, a diverse series of outcomes are possible: Civic activism may remain limited in scope and monopolized by elites; withdrawal into a private sphere of family and friends may occur; cultivation of artistic and meditative endeavors may take place; submersion of the self to the demands of bureaucratic organizations may occur; and, finally, initiative-taking may be limited exclusively to an occupation or profession. All appear possible to Weber. However, none contribute significantly to the development of a civic sphere. Moreover, according to him, a practical-ethical individualism has never crystallized alone as a consequence of inspirational speeches, purely cognitive dynamics, or philosophical movements. Rather, a *religion-based* dynamic often played an important part.

It first appeared on American soil during the Colonial era. This chapter focuses on this period. We turn now to a brief reconstruction of Weber's analysis of the origins and main features of world-mastery individualism.

World-Mastery Individualism: Religious Origins[1]

Seventeenth-century ascetic Protestantism gave birth to a particularly rigorous form of individualism, one oriented to world mastery. How did this occur according to Weber? And how did the practical-ethical individualism of these Puritans contribute to and, remarkably, become manifest in the eighteenth and nineteenth centuries as a viable civic sphere? These queries constitute focal concerns in this and the next two chapters.

An especially vigilant "watchfulness" over the creaturely impulses and desires was expected of all Puritan believers, for "right" and "wrong" were understood in rigidly moral terms, and the corrupting enticements of all pleasures were rejected to an unusual degree. However, the devout could no longer, in their quest to avoid sin, acquire assistance from sacred rituals and priests; trained intermediaries endowed with the capacity to negotiate the urgent question of salvation were now absent. Responsible exclusively to a wrathful, omniscient, Old Testament God, and standing alone before His omnipotence and vengeance, ascetic Protestants relied entirely on their inner resources to banish sin and to create "evidence" of their salvation.

These Puritans undoubtedly adhered to God's commandments as a consequence of a purely pragmatic possibility: expulsion from their religious communities. This occurrence would lead with certainty to severe social ostracism, the faithful knew (see this text, pp. 36–42). Thus, *conformity* to the religious community's standards appeared indispensable. However, Weber's sociology emphasizes also another dimension: belief. Religious faith can be sincere, conscientious, and sociologically significant, he insists. As he notes frequently, it is of course difficult for "we moderns" to imagine the urgency of the central "certainty of salvation" (*certitudo salutis*) question to sixteenth- and seventeenth-century Puritans (see Weber 2011c, pp. 123, 158, 178, 338 [n. 76]; 1985, p. 11): "am I among the saved?" Nonetheless, this difficulty should not lead sociologists to conclude that devoutness among these ascetic Protestants was absent.

The *subjective meaningfulness*[2] Puritans derived from their activity must be examined, Weber is convinced. It will then become apparent that conformity among the faithful indeed comprised only one aspect of their sincere religiosity. Another component is equally significant: their unusual and values-based, world-mastery individualism. It proved to be grounded directly in their beliefs, he maintains, and hence must be distinguished clearly from all utilitarian-based practical rationalism.

Unassisted by believers endowed with a special status and access to God—priests, bishops, cardinals, and popes—and immersed in a one-to-one relationship with their divinity, the ascetic Protestant devout stood alone before their Deity and were expected to read and interpret scripture on their own. Moreover, their wrathful, distant, and all-powerful Deity required strict adherence to His commandments; confession could not absolve human weaknesses. Finally, Puritan believers were obligated to be loyal exclusively to God, just as were Catholic monks before them. Intimate relationships in particular—even those between spouses—must assume a tone of moderation and restraint, for strong allegiances endangered *the* most important loyalty relationship.

A sturdy and self-reliant individualism grew out of this salvation ethos. However, ascetic Protestantism cultivated and even intensified this individualism in a further way, Weber holds. According to the reforms undertaken by influential Puritan divines in the seventeenth century (and, in particular, by the English pastor and writer on Puritan ethics, Richard Baxter), "activity in the world"—hard work and the search for profit—could provide believers with wealth. Moreover, riches, the Puritan divines were convinced, assisted the construction of an affluent earthly kingdom—and this abundance served to praise God's majesty and glory. However, only *some* among the industrious in fact created the wealth that rendered His kingdom prosperous—hence, the very possession of riches became viewed as a *sign* of the favoring hand of this omnipotent and omniscient God. And this Deity would offer assistance, it could be logically reasoned, only to those He had chosen—or *predestined*—to be saved.

In this manner, methodical work and the continuous search for profit, which aimed to transform the world into an abundant kingdom that would honor His glory, lost their heretofore predominantly *pragmatic and utilitarian* tenor. Instead, these activities became connected to the all-important salvation query and acquired a "psychological premium." They became *sanctified* (see Weber 1968, pp. 1199–1200, 1204–1210; 2011c, p. 258).

All activities undertaken on behalf of the accumulation of wealth now became highly acclaimed and legitimated: rugged competition, risk-taking, innovation, upward mobility, and initiative-taking. This new way of rigorously *organizing life*—to Weber, a new *ethos* or "frame of mind" (*Gesinnung*)—not only unleashed a tremendous energy that propelled a dynamic development of the economy, but also fostered a world-mastery individualism. As a means to render God's will overt, this intensified, values-oriented individualism became empowered to overcome great obstacles.

Although this "Protestant ethic" vigorously directed this practical-ethical individualism toward the ascertainment of the believer's state of grace, it also required that the devout hold others responsible for their conduct. In the new and exemplary "City on the Hill," *all* must now demonstrate allegiance to God and uphold His commandments—for in His community "weakness" must be overcome and "worldly evil" banished. A passive acceptance of the daily and random "flow of life" was prohibited; the faithful must *direct their action against* evil. Moreover, should rulers violate God's decrees, Puritan believers stood under a *religious* obligation to protest against and overthrow such "illegitimate" authority (see 2011c, pp. 115–138; 1985, p. 10; 1968, pp. 1208–1209). In these ways the devout became empowered *to act* decisively in reference to a set of beliefs:

> The ascetic conventicles and sects formed one of the most important historical foundations of modern "individualism." Their radical break away from patriarchal and authoritarian bondage, as well as *their* way of interpreting the statement that one owes more obedience to God than to man, was especially important. (2011d, p. 225, emphasis in original; see 2011a, pp. 230–232)

This brief and incomplete discussion of Weber's argument in respect to the ways in which Puritanism gave birth to a world-mastery individualism must here suffice (see Appendix II). It indicates how a set of beliefs introduced onto the American landscape a new "human being" (*Menschentyp*) endowed with a stalwart self-reliance and a readiness to reform the world on behalf of religious values and commandments. Neither cautious nor contemplative, nor accepting of either long-standing traditions or the endless utilitarian and power-anchored fluctuations of daily life, the Puritan faithful undertook to transform society as a whole. Cultivation of this disciplined, ascetic individualism occurred in the Puritan family and the self-governing congregation.

Weber emphasizes that the beliefs of the faithful encouraged activity not simply against unjust secular authority; if necessary, the devout should also act against unjust popular opinion, whether constituted from majorities or otherwise (see 1968, pp. 1208–1209; 2011a, pp. 230–231). Moreover, rigorous asceticism infused the ethical action of believers with a great intensity. The overriding importance of the "certainty of salvation" question in the seventeenth and eighteenth centuries ensured that the intense effort of the faithful to control daily activity would take God's principles and rules as their fulcrum rather than pragmatic calculations, the particular features of persons and emotional bonds with them, or popular and fashionable short-term currents (2011c, pp. 129–133; 1968, p. 578).

In sum, Weber's analysis calls attention to a type of individualism anchored *from within* by strict orientations to absolute values and principles. Capable of acting *in the world*[3] on their behalf, the Puritan at times stood even against popular opinion.[4] Remarkably, this firm individualism coexisted in ascetic Protestantism with a *belief-based* orientation to a *civic sphere*. Indeed, a symbiotic dualism congealed. We now turn to Weber's analysis of the Puritan origins of this sphere.

Community Activism: Religious Origins

At the center of the American political culture stands an enduring *tension*, Weber holds, between the world-mastery individualism just examined and an orientation of citizens toward a civic sphere. His investigations maintain that any explanation of American success at creating and sustaining civic associations on a wide scale must recognize the significant contribution of a civic realm composed of a set of specific values. These associations must be comprehended as crystallizing *in reference to this* social context, he contends. That is, characterized by distinct and conducive values-based *ideals*, the civic arena *facilitates* the birth of such groups.[5]

How did a viable civic sphere arise in the United States? Weber again calls attention to religious beliefs. He examines, first, the manner in which Puritan doctrine in the Colonial period encouraged the devout to create the kingdom of God on earth; he then investigates the unfolding of the congregation as an *ethical* community. Taken together, these eighteenth-century developments contributed in the nineteenth century to the unfolding of a thick civic realm, he argues. They created the social *context* that assisted the birth of civic associations.

Creating the Kingdom of God

Puritanism's world-mastery individualism, as noted, implied a strong orientation to the believer's salvation. It also called forth an equally strong orientation *to a community*.

The construction of God's abundant kingdom on earth constituted His will and the purpose of life for Puritans. However, rather than to be enjoyed by believers, riches must serve, through their reinvestment, God's community as a whole—for we are all His children engaged in a grand mission to enhance His glory and majesty through the creation on earth of prosperous communities in His image. Thus, purely emotional, utilitarian, or cognitive reasons never, in respect to "worldly activity," proved central; instead, religious obligations determined the conduct of the faithful. The construction of affluent communities manifestly constituted a *religious* task and a service to God.[6]

Other aspects of Puritan doctrine pushed the devout further in this direction (see also Appendix II). As discussed, individuals were left alone to discover "signs" of their predestined status. Neither a church nor its sacraments, nor holy intermediaries could address and ameliorate the extreme anxiety that accompanied uncertainty regarding one's salvation status. Nonetheless, breaking from John Calvin (1509–1564), the seventeenth-century Puritan divines offered several means of doing so. For example, if success in the world were attained, the faithful could convince themselves that their wealth itself indicated the favor of their omnipotent God: Nothing in His universe occurred by chance, and He would surely assist *only* the foreordained. And great riches might be attained by the devout only through systematic labor. Hence, unusually strong psychological premiums rewarded methodical work.[7]

Remarkably, a deepening of the believer's commitment *to a community* resulted from this intensification of work and its elevation to a central place in the lives of Puritans. Although all sought to create "evidence" of their predestined status, the means to do so—methodical labor—never served the individual alone. Instead, a firm obligation was apparent: to work on behalf of God's glory and to create the humane and abundant earthly Kingdom that extolled His majesty. Thus, labor now served—not least because these large projects required cooperation—to bind believers to a religious community. *Work in a vocation* (*Beruf*) became intensified, sanctified, and oriented to broader tasks far beyond those fulfilled by utilitarian, self-interested calculations.

Accordingly, community participation became a significant activity, one rendered all the more likely as a consequence of the ascetic Protestant congregation. This organization served as a natural training ground for the acquisition of group participation skills. In this regard, the laity's involvement in the admission of new members proved pivotal, as did the congregation's major role in selecting a righteous minister and in admonishing the "unworthy" to avoid communion—all in order strictly to ensure, as God wished, "the purity of the sacramental community" (see Weber 1968, p. 1208; 2011d, pp. 220–221, 226). As Weber notes, "The sect controlled and regulated members' conduct *exclusively* in the sense of formal *righteousness* and methodical asceticism" (2011d, p. 226; 1968, p. 1208). This milieu of trusted believers itself further facilitated the cultivation of a notion of service to the group.

A clear dualism became apparent. As discussed, a practical-ethical individualism was evident, one focused on the capacity of individuals to shape and reshape—through ethical activity and the cultivation of a goal-oriented individualism—their salvation destinies. However, an equally strong push toward engagement in a community and its improvement existed. Weber sees a "community-forming energy" imparted by the ascetic Protestant sects "to an Anglo-Saxon world" (1985, p. 11). This activism left a broad imprint on Colonial America and, as we will discuss, on the early United States.

Puritan churches placed into motion a strong thrust toward the formation of a civic sphere in another manner as well. Weber's analysis at this point emphasizes a set of further values originating from, and cultivated by, ascetic Protestantism. These values proved capable of creating an *ethical* tenor for social relationships throughout congregations; in turn, relationships in entire communities were influenced. As will be explored in Chapters 3 and 4, they paved the way for civic associations in the nineteenth century and assisted their widespread expansion.

The Ethical Community: The Congregation

According to Weber, ascetic Protestant congregations in Colonial America and the early United States gave birth to and effectively sustained candor and trust among the faithful. Members understood their activity as involving a great mission to create *communities* of believers in which *all* would be "brothers and sisters in the faith." In these organizations, trust expanded beyond its original location in the blood bond. New *family* relationships of helpfulness, allegiance, and ethical conduct, under the watchful eyes of God and the devout alike, were born among "the brethren" in congregations.

Moreover, a practical mechanism ensured that only the sincere faithful would become members of this congregation: rigid investigative procedures guaranteed that exclusively persons of "good moral character" would be admitted to this devout community of believers. Thus, membership *certified* righteous behavior, as well as a person's commitment to treat all as God's children—that is, in strict accordance with an ethos of equality and fair play (2011d, pp. 222–223; 1968, p. 1205). Hence, goodwill and openness prevailed in the congregation rather than fear, threat, insecurity, manipulation, and the brazen calculation of interests. Indeed, membership established a reputation for honesty and candor even in business relationships and even to such an extent that nonbelievers preferred to conduct commercial dealings with the devout (see Chapter 2). Fair treatment, they were convinced, would be their reward (2011d, pp. 218–219, 222–223; 1985, pp. 7–8).

In this way, carried and cultivated methodically by Puritan congregations, trust, ethical conduct, and goodwill broke from their usual location: the family tie. Attribution of these qualities became awarded to "unknown others"—as long as they were members of an ascetic Protestant congregation. Ethical conduct now became, Weber argues, comprehended as an *impersonal and binding principle*—a firm *ideal* even for commercial relationships—rather than as a strong personal relationship or a long-standing tradition (see, for example, 2011d, pp. 209–212, 218–219; 2005, pp. 284–288). As will become evident in Chapters 3 and 4, this extension of trust and ethical conduct in the seventeenth and eighteenth centuries laid the groundwork for the formation of a demarcated—and secular—*civic sphere* in the United States in the nineteenth century.

However, the Puritan ethical community contributed to the formation of a values-based civic sphere in a further significant manner: it set into motion a strong push toward community activism. A tolerance of, or separation from, evil remained unacceptable. Instead, the faithful were expected by their God to undertake a large task: a mastering of evil in the world through the creation of His Kingdom on earth. This *religious* duty firmly obligated the devout to act against evil, even if doing so challenged secular authority or popular opinion.

Thus, rather than sustaining a cautious and contemplative person, Puritanism upheld a world-mastery individualism *prepared* to undertake reform on behalf of God's will. The devout must participate in the alteration of their communities and aim to transform society as a whole—they must create the just Kingdom of God (2011c, pp.122–123, 158–175, 327 [n. 34]; 2011d, pp. 224–225; 2011a, pp. 230–232; 1968, pp. 549, 578–579, 1207–1209). Activity would be assessed in terms of its *consistency* with the principles and rules laid down by the divinity. In this manner, and although best characterized as a theocracy or quasi-theocracy, the Puritan society of the seventeenth century formulated the underlying *tracks* for the unfolding in the nineteenth century of the American civic sphere. With ascetic Protestantism the notion of improving one's community lost all utilitarian overtones; instead, it became perceived as a service to God and as part and parcel of one's religious obligation.[8]

In sum, the distinctiveness of the early American political culture can be best isolated, according to Weber, by reference to a set of religious values. Rather than rooted in emotional relationships or sheer pragmatic calculations, Puritanism's practical-ethical individualism placed abstract principles at the core of the believer's life and obligated the devout to honor them in a strict manner. Furthermore, Weber describes the American capacity to formulate groups as unusually nimble and swift. Here again he sees values and beliefs as pivotal: an array of civic values, constituted in a demarcated civic sphere, facilitated this group formation and community-building generally. As will become apparent in what follows (see Chapter 3), civic values provided a deep context and amenable pathway for this nineteenth-century development. Secularized civic associations appeared on a wide scale; indeed, their expansiveness proved unique.

Weber identified interlocking components in the early American political culture—a world-mastery, activity-oriented individualism and a community orientation broadly penetrated by a set of values—and located their original source in ascetic Protestantism.[9] Economic interests, political calculations, the power of a state, and chance occurrences all failed to explain this unusual juxtaposition, as did the use of power and the exercise of domination by cohesive groups. Uniquely American in its intensity, this *symbiotic dualism*, which stands squarely at the core of this political culture and its spirit of democracy, remains obscured by all modes of analysis that take global concepts—industrialization, modernization, value-generalization, differentiation, or evolutionary progress—as their focus, as well as by Tocqueville's master-key concept: an increasing social egalitarianism. It also remains occluded to all modes of analysis that depict the American political culture as constituted from mutually exclusive "community" and "individualism" components.

The Puritan origins of the distinctly American political culture are vividly apparent as well, Weber argues, in the social-psychological dynamic unique to the Protestant sects in the early United States. Weber insists that, in a number of ways, these sects imprinted deeply this nation's political culture. This theme captures our attention in the following chapter.

Notes

1. Appendix II offers a summary of themes salient to this section.
2. On this central Weberian expression, see the Glossary.
3. This is Weber's phrase to distinguish Puritanism from the "otherworldly" asceticism of monks "outside" the world in cloisters. "This-worldly" is used synonymously.
4. Weber here discovers a strong sociological source for the notion of the "Rights of Man" (see 1968, pp. 1208–1209; Jellinek 1979).
5. As will become apparent, Weber's explanation for the *origins* of these associations varies distinctly from that of Tocqueville. See Chapter 3, note 5.
6. Here are to be found the roots of the idea of "community service" as traditionally practiced in the United States across many age groups. Similarly, the phrase "make a contribution" even now implies an orientation beyond one's self-interests—namely, to the improvement of a community—as does the expression "service profession."
7. Weber's argument is examined in detail in Kalberg 2011a. Again, see Appendix II.
8. On the elective affinity of these (secularized) values today with a missionary foreign policy, see Kalberg 1991, 2003.

9. For a collection of important passages from Weber's scattered writings on the Puritan political culture and its influence upon the formation of the American spirit of democracy, see Weber 2005, pp. 277–289. Because many of these passages examine the ways in which the Protestant sects in America functioned as effective social carriers of theological doctrines formulated by the Puritan divines, they appropriately introduce the next chapter.

CHAPTER TWO

The Foundations II

The Protestant Sects in the American Colonies, the Early United States, and Beyond

> [The sects] … alone have been able, on the foundation of Protestantism, to instill an intensity of interest in religion in the broad middle class—and especially modern workers—that otherwise is found only, though in the form of a bigoted fanaticism, among traditional peasants.
>
> —*Weber 2011a, p. 231*

> It is crucial that sect membership meant a certificate of moral qualification and especially of business morals for the *individual*.
>
> —*Weber 2011d, p. 212; emphasis in original*

A FTER RETURNING FROM his whirlwind tour of the United States in November 1904 (see Appendix I), Weber finished *The Protestant Ethic* (*PE*) and wrote a short essay on the Protestant sects (1985). Significantly revised and expanded in 1920 (2011d), these two studies ("Sects") comment directly on the American political culture and its spirit of democracy.[1]

Less scholarly than *PE* and informal in tone, Weber seeks here to reach a much broader audience. These essays convey his perspicacious

33

observations as he travels through the New England, Midwest, Southern, and Mid-Atlantic states. His commentary, however, should not be comprehended as offering merely fragmented "impressions of American life." Instead, Weber brings his audience up to date in respect to the impact of Puritan beliefs in the United States 250 years after the landing of the Pilgrims. He focuses on two major themes.

First, he explicitly addresses the political culture of the United States. Opposing stereotypes widespread throughout Europe, and especially in Germany, Weber refuses to depict American society as a "sandpile of atoms"—of individuals adrift and without viable social and intimate connections. Rather, he sees multitudes of clubs, associations, and societies as prominent. The origins of these groups, and the vigorous engagement of their members, can be traced back to the Protestant sects, he emphasizes.

Second, *PE*'s argument is expanded in "Sects." These essays analyze how a social-psychological dynamic distinct to these organizations accomplishes two important tasks: it effectively *carries* the *ethical* action expected by Puritan ministers into the daily lives of the devout *and* transfers consistently ascetic Protestantism's economic ethic into everyday conduct. The faithful became oriented systematically to work, the search for profit, and material success as a consequence of this complex dynamic.

Weber's observations paint a picture of American society as open and energetic, yet stable. Indeed, he perceives the United States as a vibrant nation soon to embark upon a period of great power. And differences vis-à-vis European societies, he asserts, in respect to both economic and political cultures are prominent. German society in particular varied distinctly, Weber is convinced (see Chapter 4), and he attempts in "Sects" to demonstrate to his countrymen the firm and long roots of the American success story. In this respect he aims to confront—and warn against—the dismissive view of American political stability and economic power widespread among German scholars, industrialists, and politicians. Invisible to highly secularized Europeans, a distinct configuration of facilitating religious values stood at the foundation of American growth, power, wealth, and democracy, he holds.

This chapter turns first to the manner in which multitudes of Puritan sects created, especially in light of social dynamics internal to them, a political culture fundamentally characterized by "exclusivities" practiced by innumerable groups. All insulated Americans against atomistic relationships.

Weber rejected the view in Europe dominant in his era that depicted American democracy as rooted in solitary individuals (2011a, pp. 231–232; 2011d, pp. 214–219). On the contrary, multitudes of associations characterized this society, he argued: churches, sects, social clubs, hobby organizations, and varieties of political and interest groups. Americans formulated groups in an exceedingly quick and nimble fashion. Instead of a "sand heap" of unconnected and lonesome individuals, American democracy must be comprehended as grounded in "joiners," associations, and exclusivities, he insisted:

> American society in its genuine form—and here my remarks explicitly concern also the "middle" and "lower" strata—was never ... a sandpile, nor even a building where everyone who sought to enter found open, undiscriminating doors. Rather, it was, and is, saturated with "exclusivities" of all sorts. Wherever this earlier situation still remains, the individual firmly acquires a foundation under his feet, at the university and in business, only when he succeeds in being voted into a *social organization* (earlier almost without exception a church, today an organization of a different sort) and manages, within this organization, to *hold his own*. (2011a, pp. 231–232; emphasis original)

> It is still true that American democracy is not a sandpile of unrelated individuals but a maze of highly exclusive, yet absolutely voluntary, sects, associations, and clubs, which provide the center of the individual's social life. (2005, p. 287; see 2011d, pp. 216–217)

Thus, Weber emphasized an aspect of American life stressed in the strongest terms by Tocqueville: its multiple and multifarious "civic associations." They stand at the foundation of his analysis of the American political culture, its spirit of democracy, and its uniqueness.

However, unlike the French theorist, Weber locates their origins in the realm of religion.[2] Moreover, although he acknowledged that membership provided a sense of belonging and a safe foundation for activity, as had Tocqueville, he emphasized also the capacity of civic associations to bestow social honor. Rather than banished by urbanization, egalitarianism, and industrialization, social honor assumed a new form: no longer given by birth and long-standing tradition, as in feudal societies, it must be *acquired* through admission to groups widely respected in one's community (2011d, pp. 212–218; 1968, p. 933). Initiative must be taken. In search of an explanation for this foundational aspect of the American political culture, Weber investigated ascetic Protestantism's sects.

Beyond *The Protestant Ethic*: The Protestant Sect

PE offers a detailed portrait of the Puritan cosmos of belief and the contours of the meaningful action found among the devout. By reference to the doctrine of Predestination and revisions undertaken by Richard Baxter and other Puritan divines, Weber's classic study provides an explanation for the world-mastery asceticism of the faithful and their intense orientation to God. The solitary salvation quest, pursued by the believer without assistance from church intermediaries and despite the fatalism implied by the Predestination decree, stands at the center of his discussion (see 2011c, pp. 118–122). Through a fine-grained analysis, *PE* explores the eventual attachment of subjective meaning and ethical standards to certain practical and economic activities, as well as to a disciplined and organized life. The "psychological rewards" placed on action by this Puritanism remain prominent. These large themes dominate his massive inquiry into the Protestant ethic's origins (see Appendix II).

In the course of the eighteenth century, the process of "testifying" to one's salvation status assumed significant new dimensions for the ascetic devout. It moved away from lonely attempts by the faithful to orient their activities to God and to create "evidence" of their salvation, Weber holds, and toward groups of believers situated deeply within a *social* milieu—namely, in the American *Protestant sect*.[3] Hence, he now expands his analysis beyond *PE*'s question—how can the faithful prove their sincerity *before God?*—to an investigation of how the devout testify to their belief *before men* (2011d, pp. 225–226). Although believers drew upon an internal strength in order to lead "the moral life" and remain focused on God, the sect's strict monitoring and unrelenting conformist pressure also significantly influenced the activity of members, Weber now argues.

This tightly knit group cultivated and strengthened the doctrinal-based ethical action and methodical-rational organization of life originally expected of believers by the Puritan divines. Thus, "Sects" explores how ideas and values are efficiently "implemented," owing to the impact of the Protestant sect. By inculcating the beliefs and psychological rewards enunciated by the Puritan cosmos, this social carrier of values, as a firm organization, confirmed ethical conduct and conveyed it *systematically* to believers. How did the sect do so?

Weber's pivotal distinction between "sect" and "church" must be noted. We will then be prepared to consider his multivalent, social-psychological analysis of the sectarian origins of American society's multitude of civic associations. We can then also perceive their capacity to orient the activity of members in a *practical-ethical* direction (see Chapter 3).

Sect and Church

A church implies to Weber an inclusive, "sacred corporation." Members are born into it. As a "universal institution" and a "trust fund of eternal blessings ... offered to everyone," the church allows its "grace [to] shine over all"—the righteous and unrighteous alike. This organization officially monopolizes and mediates all sacred values on behalf of a "universalism of grace" (2011d, p. 212; 1968, p. 1164).

Its task—to cultivate religious beliefs and conduct, and to save each member's soul—often proves difficult. Because obligatory, church membership never implies that individuals possess special spiritual and ethical qualities. Even sinners and heretics are included, owing to this organization's encompassing democratic mission. However, its laity possesses a lesser faith than its priests, and their elevated position in an elaborate hierarchy grants to them a special aura, or "office charisma." Hence, they possess a clear authority to subject the sinner to the church's discipline and to address all salvation concerns and specific violations. Through the confessional, priests are guardians of the church's "trust fund" and endowed with the capacity to assess the "ethical sufficiency of all those ... enrolled under [its] institutional authority" (2011a, p. 229; see 1968, p. 1164; 1946e, p. 288).

Sects, as voluntary communities composed exclusively of persons with demonstrated "religious qualifications," diverge distinctly. Admission occurs only after a probationary period in which the candidate's sincerity of belief and moral character are clearly scrutinized. This examination *must* take place, sect members insist, for God's majesty would be insulted and dishonored by the presence of the sinful at the Lord's Supper. His wrath will strike unless the "qualified [are separated] from the unqualified" (1968, pp. 1204–1206); the "black sheep" must be excluded. Were debts promptly paid? Were visits to a tavern frequent? Dancing? Was card-playing or gambling evident among admission candidates? Were the childhood years disorderly? Because a sincerity of character must be evident, a wide-ranging investigation proved indispensable. Potential members must have avoided frivolities, flaws, and blemishes (2011d, pp. 211–212; 1968, pp. 1205–1206).

Moreover, the conviction of sect members that God must be obeyed—and strictly—more than men, places a clear demand upon behavior. It must be unequivocally oriented to God's will and in full accord with the sacred Word—it must be "righteous." The entire sect, acting as a firm community and on behalf of appropriate conduct, disciplined its members. On the other hand, churches disciplined in an authoritarian manner through the clergy (1968, pp. 1204–1205).

Thus, sect members view themselves as belonging to a religious elite.[4] "Ethical purity" and a capacity to live "the clean life" constitute central concerns among the devout, and exemplary conduct must be displayed in the "visible church" (2011d, pp. 212, 218–219; 2011a, pp. 229–230). Finally, outside a "salvation institution" and severed from religious officials empowered to administer special means of dispensation, believers are left entirely on their own:

> The idea that the individual, on the basis of the religious quali-
> fications bestowed upon him by God, decided on his salvation

status exclusively on his own was important.... Only the believer's practical conduct mattered: his behavior "proved and testified" to his faith and alone provided a *sign* that he stood on the road to salvation. (2005, pp. 285–286; emphasis in original)

On account of these variations, churches and sects influenced the action of believers in quite differing ways, Weber concludes.[5] More effective in instilling sincere faith, the sect disciplined the devout to a unique degree of intensity on behalf of an ethical posture, he contends—all the more so owing to the absence of a forgiving priest with a direct connection to God's mercy. Heterogeneous social-psychological dynamics were at work here. The far greater capacity of sects to mold and shape activity—to "breed" *ethical* qualities—is a theme of pivotal centrality to Weber. Because it underlies major elements of his analysis of the American political culture and its spirit of capitalism, it constitutes our next concern.

The Sect's Social-Psychological Dynamic: "Holding Your Own" Individualism, Conformity, and the Methodical-Rational Organization of Life

High standards and strict ethical codes must be upheld by all sect members. Weber argues that this organization's strong influence over the faithful became manifest in several ways. It offered an array of significant contributions to the American political culture and its spirit of democracy.

First, as a consequence of selective admission procedures, sect membership itself legitimized and guaranteed one's good character. Combined with the believer's focus on God, this "certificate of moral qualification" clearly defined every transgression: a "fall from grace" had occurred rather than a random and forgivable lapse. The sect, however, having banished Catholicism's mechanism—the confession—to address sinfulness, lacked institutionalized means to relieve internal distress (2011d, pp. 211–212, 224–225). A qualitative strengthening of the necessity for the faithful to act *constantly* in a righteous manner resulted, according to Weber.

Second, the sect's self-governing feature also enhanced its remarkable capacity to call forth ethical activity. The exercise of discipline and authority in this group was distinct from their exercise in churches: although less centralized and authoritarian in the sects, because now in the hands of laymen, discipline and authority became for this reason more thorough and encompassing, according to Weber (2011d, pp. 221–222). Any misstep would surely be revealed.[6]

Third, the definition of the American sect as an "exclusive" organization of pure believers implied that expulsion would follow immediately upon any exposure of "poor character." This harsh treatment involved an intolerable situation for the expelled, Weber emphasizes: through its innumerable activities (church suppers, Sunday school, charitable activities, team sports, Bible study groups, etc.), the sect not only efficiently shaped the conduct of members and thereby bestowed arrays of psychological premiums on appropriate socialization, but also monopolized the believer's social life. Those excluded for "dishonorable conduct" immediately "[suffered] ... a kind of social boycott" and a collapse of their entire social existence (2011d, pp. 222, 224–225; 2005, pp. 287–288; 1968, p. 1206). The necessity to "hold one's own" under the watchful eyes of peers—to testify unceasingly through ethical conduct to one's membership among the elect—now became intensified, as did the sect's capacity to mold action: "The most powerful individual interest of social self-esteem [was put] in the service of this breeding of traits" (2011c, p. 222).[7]

Fourth, Weber refers to a related social-psychological dynamic to explain further the unique capacity of the Protestant sects to cultivate and sustain ethical activity. The faithful, as a consequence of the selection of members on the basis of moral qualities, were viewed as persons of great integrity and even trustworthiness within their geographical regions. As the sect—largely for this reason—acquired social prestige, supervision of behavior among the devout became further intensified: now the sect's favorable reputation throughout a community must be maintained. In other words, to the degree that social honor within the larger community became salient, members became subject to enhanced conformity pressures to uphold "good moral character" standards.

A shaping of an ethical posture also took place in this manner, Weber contends. Indeed, by engaging the entire person and bestowing both social honor and esteem,[8] sects had the effect—especially in contrast to the authoritarianism of churches—of disciplining believers to cultivate ethical action to a unique degree of intensity: "According to all experience there is no stronger means of breeding traits than through the necessity of holding one's own in the midst of one's associates" (2011d, p. 224; see pp. 219–220; 1968, p. 1206). Weber saw here a source of American initiative-taking vis-à-vis standards and the American notion of self-respect.

Fifth, and finally, the sect constituted a functional, even "impersonal" (*sachliche*) group: rather than oriented to each other, members were above all oriented *to tasks* that serve God's greater glory and assist the construction of His Kingdom. By promoting "the precise ordering of the individual into the instrumental task pursued by the group," this "mechanism for the achievement of ... material and ideal goals" circumscribed affect-laden and tradition-laden relationships among the faithful. Neither emotion-based interaction prevailed in the sect[9] nor did a warm and sentimental mode rooted in familiar and long-standing traditions.[10] In addition, all residue of any "mystical total essence floating above [the believer] and enveloping him" was banished (2011c, p. 337, n. 34; 2005, p. 286).[11]

A halo never encompassed the sect—one into which the devout could merge amid a sacred glow. Rather, an orientation by the individual to tasks in service to God and high standards of ethical conduct reigned. Stalwart believers, evaluated exclusively by reference to the "religious qualities evident in [their] conduct," constantly attended to the necessity of holding their own (2011a, p. 232; 2005, p. 286). According to Weber, and despite the typically intense interaction among sect members, a cultivation of deep emotional ties with others and an immersion into the group failed to occur. "Association" (*Vergesellschaftung*) with others, and sociability, characterized interaction.[12]

In sum, in juxtaposing an unceasing orientation to activities, tasks, ethical standards, and intense conformity pressures with a hold-your-own individualism, sects pulled the devout away from emotion-oriented relationships, tradition-oriented sentimentality, and all tendencies to attribute a sacred aura to groups. However, far from abandoning believers to the flux and flow of a daily life, interest-oriented and power-oriented practical rationalism, or to an endless random and nihilistic drift, the sect immediately took firm hold of the faithful. The devout now became tightly bound within its social-psychological dynamic—one that actively cultivated, sustained, and rejuvenated the ethical action at the foundation of the American spirit of democracy.

Weber's position must be repeated. The *methodical-rational* organization of life typically found among ascetic Protestants arose in part from the individual's lonely quest to create "evidence" of his salvation and the psychological rewards placed on ethical action by the Puritan divines, as charted in *PE*. However, it also can be seen as originating from the social dynamic in the Protestant sect. Indeed, the requirement of this group—to ensure that only the morally qualified participate in communion—can be understood as itself providing an impetus to the congregation's many social activities, for they enabled the indispensable monitoring of members' conduct.[13] To Weber, "The sect and its derivations are one of [America's] unwritten but vital constitutional elements, since they shape the individual more than any other influence" (1968, p. 1207). And,

> The Puritan sects put the most powerful *individual* interest of social self-esteem in the service of [a] breeding of traits. Hence *individual* motives and personal self-interests were also placed in the service of maintaining and propagating the "middle class" Puritan ethic, with all its ramifications. This is absolutely decisive for its penetrating and for its powerful effect. (2011d, pp. 224–225; emphasis in original)

Integrating values—universalism, fairness, and trustworthiness—became the standards for community-wide ethical behavior in regions where these ascetic Protestant sects became dominant. Ethical values, now carried by cohesive organizations, penetrated into—and transformed—the calculating, practical-rational relationships often predominant in the political and economic arenas. As will become apparent in the following chapter, a value-based *civic* realm here found its origin in the American political culture. This aspect of the American spirit of democracy stood firm against practical rationalism (Weber 2011d; 2011a; 1968, pp. 1205–1206).

The Puritan Sects: Democratic Governance, Freedom of Conscience, and the Opposition to Secular Authority

Weber connects two achievements of the Puritan political culture to the active formation of, and participation in, civic associations in the nineteenth and twentieth centuries. First, the ascetic Protestant congregation practiced a mode of broad self-governance that strongly contributed to an expansion—albeit often severed from this religious root—of participatory democracy in the nineteenth century:

> In contrast to all consistent churches, all rigorous sects adhere to the principle of lay preaching and of every member's priesthood.... Moreover, pure sects also insist upon "direct democratic administration" by the congregation and upon treating the clerical officials as servants of the congregation. These very structural features demonstrate the elective affinity between the sect and political democracy. (1968, p. 1208)

Second, owing to a particularly strict rendering of the decree to "obey God more than men," the Puritan sects and churches opposed vehemently any developments in the direction of a "charisma of office"; here, a special halo of legitimacy and respect surrounded secular authority. However, convinced that rulers as well are sinners, ascetic Protestants argued that *human* authority must be condemned as idolatry, or as a deification of human wants and desires. Asceticism always demonstrates, according to Weber, hostility to authority—and this feature constitutes "the historical foundation for the uniqueness, even today, of the *democracy* among peoples influenced by Puritanism" (2011c, pp. 365–366; emphasis in original). To the seventeenth-century Puritan divine Richard Baxter, "the great danger exists, in attributing both authority and respect, that eventually the obedience to *God* will thereby be endangered" (2011c, p. 329, n. 39).[14] Moreover, ascetic Protestants believed that, should rulers violate God's decrees, the faithful stood under a *religious* obligation to protest against and overthrow such illegitimate and unjust authority (see 2011a, pp. 230–231; 1968, pp. 1208–1209).[15]

In sum, both in terms of its doctrine and the sect dynamic it called forth, Puritanism empowered the devout to act decisively in the political realm on behalf of a set of rules and principles. Required by religious belief, the devout *must* take action against secular authority and popular opinion. The idea of the rights of individuals could then flourish:

> The consistent sect gives rise to an inalienable personal right of the governed as against any power, whether political, hierocratic or patriarchal. Such freedom of conscience may be the oldest Right of Man.... The other Rights of Man or civil rights were joined to this basic right. (1968, p. 1209, see p. 1207; 1996, pp. 40–41; 2011d, p. 225; 2011a, pp. 231–232)[16]

Weber emphasizes in particular the influence of this spirit of democracy rooted in the Protestant sects on the American political culture of the eighteenth century. He also stresses, however, that these groups cast a long and expansive shadow. Its contours become quite visible in the nineteenth century. This crucial century must now be addressed. The following two chapters examine this longer-term influence of the early American spirit of democracy.

Notes

1. *PE* focuses on a religious doctrine and a religious tradition dominant in the United States. For the most part, Weber poured his observations regarding the effects of ascetic Protestantism upon American society generally (beyond the predominant work ethic) largely into these essays, as soon will become apparent. For the unabridged essays, see Weber 1985; 2002, pp. 127–147. See also Weber 2005, pp. 277–289.
2. On Tocqueville on these origins, see Chapter 3, note 5.
3. "The major domicile of the sects is the United States" (1968, p. 1206).
4. "The sect is a group whose very nature and purpose precludes universality and requires the free consensus of its members, since it aims at being an aristocratic group, an association of persons with full religious qualification" (1968, p. 1204). See Glossary.
5. In the American eighteenth century, Baptists, Quakers, Methodists, Mennonites, and Presbyterians (Calvinists) all constituted sects, according to Weber.

6. This feature of the sect in particular lends to it, Weber contends, a monitoring capacity that rivals that of the monastic order. See 2011d, pp. 222–225.

7. "Hold one's own" is the usual translation of *sich behaupten*. It implies, within a constituted group, a maintenance and defense of an individual's social—and ethical—standing vis-à-vis one's peers. "Prove your mettle" conveys today the same idea in secularized and routinized forms, as does the notion that persons should "measure up" to the task at hand. Although *within* a tightly knit group, members never "lose themselves" or "dissolve into" the group; rather, and despite intense interaction that otherwise would ensure an orientation exclusively to others, a focus by each member on an ethical standard remains (see 2011d, p. 232). Although an unequivocally positive connotation is awarded to "holding your own" in the United States, persons from cultures uninfluenced by this tradition of world-mastery asceticism may well view this degree of individualism with skepticism—namely, as dangerously close to egocentrism.

8. Those who conducted themselves in an exemplary fashion according to the expectations of sect members received from them a clear message: you are honorable and accepted. This unmediated bestowal of social esteem must have served to elevate the devout psychologically and to counterbalance any residual inclination toward fatalism stemming from the doctrine of Predestination. Interestingly, whereas the religious context here determined that approval from one's fellows implied a symbolic dimension ("you are saved"), cohesive groups in the American twentieth century could bestow only the *caput mortuum*, or routinized, form of approval: "you are well liked." This tension between the person in search of approval (and hence conforming to group norms) and the person holding his own inside the group by adhering to ethical standards endures in American society to the present. See Chapter 6.

9. In this regard Weber notes Puritanism's condemnation of all deification of personal wants and desires (*Kreaturvergötterung*)—for their satisfaction competes with the believer's loyalty to God—as denying legitimacy to a focus on the person and all privatized concerns. See 2011c, pp. 327–329, n. 39; Kalberg 2012, pp. 291–300.

10. Toennies's famous *Gemeinschaft-Gesellschaft* (1957) dichotomy was well-known to Weber. He is here explicitly taking an antagonistic position (see 2011a, p. 232), as he does throughout his works.

11. Weber has here in mind both Catholicism and Lutheranism. Because enveloped by a mystical aura, members of these churches are absolved of an urgent necessity to hold their own. He is critical of this mode of group formation, which he found to be widespread in the Germany of his time (see Mommsen 1974, pp. 80–81).

12. "Sociation" also offers an adequate translation of *Vergesellschaftung*.

13. Unmentioned in Weber's texts, this point has been inferred.

14. On Baxter's view that the belief in authority is sinful, see this note further.

15. Weber points out a direct contrast to Lutheranism: after the Peasant War (1524–1525), Luther upheld a position that failed to empower subjects. According to him, rulers must abide by God's commandments. However, if they fail to do so, subjects were not bound as a matter of religious duty to overthrow this unjust rulership. Rather, God will hold the ruler responsible.

16. Weber further notes the focus of Puritans on belief rather than either conformity to group pressure or obedience to authority: "The exclusive appraisal of a person purely in terms of the religious qualities evidenced in his conduct necessarily prunes feudal-dynastic romanticism from its roots" (2011a, p. 230). On the religious origins of the American Bill of Rights, see Jellinek (1979). On Jellinek's influence on Weber, see Bendix and Roth (1971, pp. 308–310).

CHAPTER THREE

The "Eminent Power" of the American Political Culture to Form Groups

From Sects to Civic Associations, the Civic Sphere, and Practical-Ethical Action in the Nineteenth Century

The significance of the sects expands beyond the realm of religion. American democracy, for example, acquired its own dynamic form and unique imprint exclusively from them.

—Weber 2011a, p. 231

American society ... was never ... a sandpile, nor even a building where everyone who sought to enter found open and similar doors. Rather, it was, and is, saturated with "exclusivities" of all sorts. Wherever this earlier situation still remains, the individual firmly acquires a foundation under his feet, at the university and in business, only when he succeeds in being voted into a *social organization*.

—Weber 2011a, pp. 231–232; emphasis in original

THE PROTESTANT ETHIC began to lose its religious foundation in many regions as early as the middle of the eighteenth century, according to Weber. Represented by Benjamin Franklin, a "spirit of capitalism" gradually took its place—namely, a configuration of secular values directly indebted to Puritanism. The supernatural justification heretofore pivotal had been stripped from this spirit.[1]

Nonetheless, the "sect spirit" lived on throughout the nineteenth century, Weber argues, its values, internal dynamics, and spirit of democracy now cultivated and carried by a great variety of clubs, societies, and associations. He saw, for example, the many business groups pervasive in the United States, such as the Lions, Rotary, and Kiwanis associations, as direct legacies. Membership, which occurred through similar selection processes ("balloting") and involved a close monitoring of behavior, constituted a "badge of respectability" in a community that testified to one's moral character and social honor as a "gentleman" (Weber 2009, pp. 191–194; 1968, pp. 1206–1207):[2]

> The modern position of the secular clubs and societies with recruitment by ballot is largely the product of a process of *secularization*. Their position is derived from the far more exclusive importance of the prototype of these voluntary associations, to wit, the *sects*. (Weber 2011d, pp. 217–218; emphasis in original)

> Large numbers of "orders" and clubs of all sorts have begun to assume in part the functions of the religious group. Almost every small businessman who thinks something of himself wears some kind of badge in his lapel. However, the archetype of this form, which *all* use to guarantee the "honorableness" of the individual, is indeed the ecclesiastical community. (Weber 2005, p. 288, translation altered, emphasis in original; see 2011d, p. 214)

Innumerable and multifarious groups distinguished this political culture. Multiple "exclusivities" characterized its spirit of democracy rather than "sandpiles" of unconnected individuals, Weber holds. How did these groups originate? Puritanism must be acknowledged as the deep cultural and long-term source of this unusual capacity to form groups and contain atomization, he contends. How did this transformation in the nineteenth century from Protestant sects to secular groups take place? And how did this alteration introduce and carry *practical-ethical* action—indeed, a civic individualism—into the American political culture on a broad scale?

This chapter addresses three major themes: (a) the "eminent power" of ascetic Protestantism to form groups; (b) the origin and features of an American civic sphere that nourished practical-ethical activity; and (c) the ways in which the Puritan sects, as a consequence of a generalization of their values in the nineteenth century into schools, neighborhoods, and communities, became transformed into civic associations. With these developments, the American spirit of democracy acquires significant new components.

This demarcated *realm*—a civic sphere—helped the American political culture to sustain a capacity to form innumerable groups of varying composition, Weber argues, thereby effectively confronting sandpile atomization. Its origin must be located primarily in the ecclesiastical community rather than rational choices, network dynamics, the state, political and economic interests, and macrostructural, overarching modernization transformations, Weber insists. The capacity of this delimited arena to place in motion a significant thrust toward group formation will be first summarized.

"American Society Is Not a Sandpile"

As noted in Chapter 1, the purpose of Puritan devotion—to serve God by creating His noble and righteous Kingdom on earth—oriented the faithful away from personal interests and desires and toward this supreme being. Loyalty to His purposes must prevail, and the devout must monitor this allegiance. Moreover, because behavior deemed ethical testified to "God's strength within" and therefore to a favorable salvation status (for He would not favor with His energy just anyone), the saved recognized a common sincerity and trustworthiness. On this basis their association with one another occurred without force or fear, and hence the formation of congregations was facilitated: "This very notion—the individual could testify to his salvation through his righteous behavior—formulated the foundation for the social knitting together of the congregation" (Weber 2011a, p. 231). "[Puritan] individualism," Weber maintains, "produced an eminent power to form *groups*" (2005, p. 284; translation altered):

> The tying together of the internal isolation of the individual (which means that a maximum of his energy is deployed externally) with his ability to form social groups having the most stable cohesion and maximum impact at first was realized most fully on the soil of the formation of the sects. (Weber 2005, p. 285; translation altered)[3]

For these reasons, believers began distinctly to turn away from a cultivation of the private realm's deep personal relationships. A veritable circumscribing of the emotions followed, Weber argues.[4] To the same extent, a focusing upon impersonal tasks occurred more easily, as did cooperation—for persons shared a purpose and activities. And individuals oriented to common aims fit better into groups than individuals immersed in the emotions, Weber contends. "Groups became mechanisms" operating on behalf of *goals*. Moreover, they acquired legitimacy and prestige, owing to their overarching aim: to build God's Kingdom. Thus, individuals experienced a clear pressure to conform to the group. In turn, the believer's "dedication to the group" further enhanced integration (2009, pp. 107–108, 492 [n. 34], 204, 493–494 [n. 39]).

Once formed, this dynamic became self-sustaining, Weber holds. In addition, the purposive and impersonal mode of interaction that prevailed among the devout facilitated the important focus on tasks; indeed, it promoted the "precise ordering" of the individual into the group's agenda despite regular, and even intense, emotional interaction (2011a, p. 232).

Finally, this "sociation" mode (*Vergesellschaftung*) assisted social lubrication, a continued orientation by the faithful to ethical standards, and a regular surveillance of sect members' behavior—thereby enabling the sect's concern with the ethical responsibility of individuals to move further to the forefront. The trusting and "respectable" deportment of the faithful was intensified, as was group solidarity. A self-sustaining cycle was placed into motion, indeed one that contributed directly to the American political culture and its spirit of democracy.

In this manner, the systematic orientation of believers *to the super-natural realm* unexpectedly cultivated, among initiative-taking individuals, *practical* developments. Innumerable groups and extensive group-forming skills were fostered in the Colonial era. All explanations for the extensive capacity of Americans to form groups that focus exclusively on the utilitarian and pragmatic concerns of persons in the immediate present, Weber concludes, must be rejected.[5] Furthermore, rather than disappearing under the onslaught of homogenizing industrialization and urbanization, the "old sect spirit" lived on; despite secularization, it remained highly influential in the nineteenth century, he argues. A religion-based transformation occurred: the congregation's values, ideals, and social dynamics expanded into communities generally. Owing to these unusual group-formation capacities, the American political culture never assumed the form of a "sandpile of unconnected individuals" (2005, p. 286).

The Expansion of the Congregation's Values into Communities and the Formation of a Civic Sphere

The values carried by the Protestant sects penetrated throughout entire communities. They remained influential, Weber contends, even as they became weakened with secularization. Now cultivated by families, schools, neighborhoods, civic organizations, social groups, and communities generally, those values of the American political culture that located their origins in the religion domain spread far and wide.

Community-wide standards became articulated. Although social activists in the nineteenth century seldom viewed their engagement as "doing God's work," or as designed to acquire a Deity's favor through a confrontation with evil and the creation of an ethical community on earth, they were rewarded with the esteem of their community, as were their predecessors. Membership in a civic association, now a mark of social honor rather than of devoutness, bestowed a "status elevation."[6] Indeed, full acceptance in one's community and upward mobility required this membership. It alone certified a person's "good conduct" and trustworthiness (see Weber 2011d, pp. 217–219; 1985, pp. 7–8; 1968, p. 1207).

Innumerable clubs, societies, and associations in the nineteenth century evaluated the behavior of applicants and selected by ballot those of good moral character. Once granted membership, the individual, vis-à-vis the group's ethical standards, must *hold his own* under the "watchful eyes" of his fellows. And membership, as had admission into the sect, signified a claim to respectability, decency, and status. To Weber, "American democracy is not a sandpile of unrelated individuals, but a maze of highly exclusive yet absolutely voluntary sects, associations and clubs which provide the center of the individual's social life" (1968, p. 1207). Rather than "the open door," exclusivities permeated this nation's political culture and spirit of democracy. To a great extent, this "tremendous flood of social groupings" accounts for its uniqueness (2011a, pp. 231–232).

As social relationships oriented to candor, honesty, fair play, and "good conduct" expanded, *civic ideals* came into being. Wherever prominent, public life could be observed and evaluated by reference to these values. Arrays of distinct, even ethical, secular ideals for public life—a civic *realm*—crystallized in the early United States. This arena of goodwill and trust proved agreeable and welcoming rather than harsh and authoritarian—and even capable of "pulling" citizens into civic associations.[7] Their creation, in other words, was strongly facilitated by these ideals; once in place, they also legitimated these groups.

As ideals of public ethics, the legacies of ascetic Protestantism—a "sect spirit" that held "sway with relentless effect in the internal character of these organizations" (Weber 2011a, p. 232)—created in this manner community-wide norms of ethical standards, participation, and service—that is, a *civic sphere*. Weber's analysis locates its source and substance in this religious tradition and its social carriers: the Puritan churches and sects. A *social milieu*—civic activism and civic ideals—became established in the later eighteenth and early nineteenth centuries that proved indispensable for the development of civic associations on a wide scale, he maintained. This civic arena formed a context amenable to the formation of these groups. Weber repeatedly called attention to the causal significance of these Puritan legacies for an understanding of this political culture's proclivity to formulate such associations on a broad scale.[8] For example,

It is obvious that in all these points the modern functions of American sects and sect-like associations ... are revealed as straight derivatives, rudiments, and survivals of those conditions which once prevailed in all ascetic sects and conventicles. (2011d, p. 223, see also pp. 210–212, 215–217, 224–225)

The tremendous flood of social groups, which penetrate all corners of American life, is constituted according to this "sect" model. (Weber 2011a, p. 231)[9]

In this way, Weber explains the formation in the early United States of a demarcated civic sphere substantially endowed with an array of influential values. Although innumerable exclusive associations are characteristic, discrete groups located randomly in a public realm separate from the state, the family, and business corporations never constituted the American civic arena. Furthermore, Weber insists vehemently that this sphere never congealed from utilitarian and pragmatic calculations alone. Rather, a value-based and consistent *foundation* for these organizations had been efficiently provided by the realm of religion: a specific constellation of religious values proved central to the formation of this arena and its longer-term survival, Weber argues. To him, these values stood at the core of the expansive and vigorous dynamic of group-formation that distinguished the American political culture's spirit of democracy.

An explanation of the unusual propensity of Americans to formulate associations cannot rest alone upon reference to commercial and political groups, freedom and free institutions, the idea that the nation's destiny lies in the hands of its citizens, or a realization that the furtherance of one's private interests are connected to the public prosperity, Weber contends, for these elements have existed in political cultures in which civic associations have remained rare.[10] Rather, these groups are formed on a broad scale only if *facilitating civic values* anchored in a viable *civic sphere* have created an amenable deep cultural context for their creation and development, he maintains. And, to the extent that civic groups and the ideals of a civic sphere influence social relationships, other relationships oriented to power, domination, the calculation of interests, and conventions anchored in rigid social hierarchies are to the same degree called into question, he holds.[11]

The Maintenance of Public Ideals and Civic Ethics: "Practical-Ethical Action" and the New Symbiotic Dualism

In the form of *ideals* of universal justice, fair play, social trust, and equal opportunity, integrating values endured as "public ideals" and "civic ethics" in the American political culture. Despite empirical abuse and violation on a regular basis, they remained behavioral yardsticks that perpetually reinvigorated *hopes* among citizens for ethical action in economic and political relationships. In doing so—on occasion and at times decisively—they empowered citizens to act on behalf of their fulfillment. These integrating civic values, as will be discussed in Chapter 6, are visible even today, albeit in far less intense manifestations.[12]

The salience of civic ideals and a civic sphere in the American spirit of democracy can be illustrated from yet another angle. Assisted by a broad emphasis on personal liberties and the limited tasks of governance, ethical action acquired an unusual *location*—namely, beyond its accustomed home in family relationships yet fully disassociated from political authorities and the state (see Weber 1985, pp. 10–11). Innumerable civic associations carried and spread—with inestimable consequences—this "practical-ethical" action across American society's political and economic arenas. Cultivated in demarcated groups, this civic-oriented action repeatedly, and occasionally in a widespread manner, challenged and restricted the sheer utilitarian, practical-rational motivations common to the political and economic domains, Weber maintains (see 2011a, pp. 230–232; 1985, p. 11). At times, the civic values implied by practical-ethical action permeated and altered these spheres, thereby extending and rejuvenating a specifically American version of social trust and community building. Indeed, whenever this expansion occurred, even into arenas including the criminal justice system, the state and its laws oriented activities as secondary mechanisms only.[13]

Moreover, and although characterized by a significant capacity to tame and direct individualism toward the ideals of the American civic sphere, a state of tension infused this political culture and its spirit of democracy: its "individual" and "civic" components, although grounded in a common religious origin and inextricably intertwined, strained in opposite directions and clashed repeatedly. However, these conflicts were far from random; rather, they ranged across a firmly bounded spectrum. Pendulum movements too far in one direction became subject to countervailing forces.

This tension-filled dualism itself significantly injected the dynamism into the American political culture so admired by Weber. If a prominent civic sphere had been lacking, value-infused, world-mastery individualism would long ago have become routinized into a practical-rational activity characterized by the sheer calculation of interests. Ultimately, massive cynicism would stand at the end of such a development—in respect to *both* the realm of politics and the realm of ethical action generally. However, directed by a *civic orientation* rooted ultimately in the goal of the seventeenth and eighteenth centuries to create God's Kingdom on earth, this asceticism-rooted individualism became transformed in the nineteenth century into a practical-ethical, "civic individualism."[14] Had this element been lacking, a widespread and oppressive social conformism would have expanded and long ago called forth severe social, political, and economic stagnation.[15] Just the endurance of this tension between these interwoven components of the American political culture implied that a mechanism for dynamic rejuvenation remained in place. A *symbiotic dualism* was characteristic.[16]

In sum, Weber's analysis unveils an array of long-term causal factors. Indeed, he weaves historical legacies often occluded into the core of his argument. Values and beliefs proved influential, as well as their social carriers: Puritan sects and churches in the seventeenth and eighteenth centuries and civic associations in the nineteenth century. In other words, Weber focuses, on the one hand, on the manner in which the subjective meaning of persons in groups establishes firm patterns of action—including value-based and belief-based regularities—and on the other hand, on the particular groups that served as the bearers of these patterns of action. If carried by powerful organizations, these patterns cast their imprint across the ages. Indeed, as legacies, they did

so even when monumental transformations—secularization, urbanization, and industrialization, for example—substantively altered their
social carriers.

Notes

1. Again, see Appendix II for details on "the Protestant ethic thesis."
2. Hence, "the gentleman" can be seen as a secularized version of "the
saved."
3. The "internal isolation of the individual" resulted from the abolition
of the confession and the priest's intermediary position between God and the
devout, both of which enabled direct assistance to the faithful regarding the
certainty of salvation question and religious devotion in general. The resulting
relationship between the divinity and ascetic Protestant believers was direct
yet asymmetrical. It was also impersonal, owing to the centrality of universal
commandments and the believer's clear tasks rather than qualities of the
individual believer. And the devout were convinced that *this* relationship far
outweighed any other. Furthermore, because the faithful are aware that an
internal quest in search of answers to the certainty of salvation query remains a
futile endeavor, energy is, to a maximum degree, deployed externally—toward
activity. A certain impoverishment of the spiritual realm results.
4. For a more detailed discussion of the manner in which this occurred,
see Kalberg 2012, pp. 291–300.
5. This is Tocqueville's focus. The centrality of civic associations in his
analysis poses an urgent question: How did the Americans manage to form
them with such "extreme skill" and "nimbleness"? He sees the first impulse
toward their formation as deriving from the realm of commerce. Common
economic interests, he asserts, draw people together into associations. As such
"small affairs" multiply, persons acquire experience in coming together as a
consequence of common interests. A facility in doing so is born (see 1945,
vol. 2, p. 123). As it develops, this facility carries over into the formation
of groups with political goals. In turn, political associations effectively give
sustenance to civic associations. As the "knowledge of public life" increases,
"the notion of associations and the wish to coalesce present themselves" and
"political life makes the love and practice of association more general" (vol. 2,
pp. 123–125, 127, 251–252; see also vol. 2, pp. 111–113, 252). Hence, from
the political realm itself there arises "a desire of union." See Kalberg 1997,
pp. 211–218. On the role of self-interests in the development of patriotism,
civic zeal, and the authority of the law, according to Tocqueville, see 1945,
vol. 1, pp. 250–253, 256–257; see also generally Crèvecoeur (1981).

6. Hence, a formal parallel exists here to Weber's argument regarding the relationship between the Protestant ethic and the spirit of capitalism (see 2011c, pp. 108–109, 177–179): in both cases the religious roots had died out.

7. Here can be seen, as well as the trust cultivated among believers in the congregation, one of the sources for the uniquely widespread belief in America (outside the Old South) in populism, or trust in the good judgment and basic wisdom of the common person.

8. The extreme importance of admission into a community's churches and clubs for one's social status led Weber to describe the United States as a society of "benevolent feudalism." Although this "feudalism" lacked the European social hierarchies and domination by a closed class, it retained feudalism's typical emphasis on social status. See 1978, p. 281.

9. "[Religious institutions are] the most characteristic features of American life, as well as the most fateful factors for a deep inner transformation. Up to now it was the orthodox sects here that gave to all of life its special character. All sociability, all social cohesion, all agitation in favor of philanthropic and ethical and even political concerns (such as the campaign against corruption) are held in their grasp" (Letter of September 20, 1904, from the United States; from Scaff 1998, p. 66).

10. This is a short listing of the elements Tocqueville defines as causal forces behind the American propensity to form civic associations. See note 5 above.

11. Given the strength of these opposing social relationships, Weber is quite well aware that often these ideals had little actual impact (see Chapter 6). That ideals are not always upheld—indeed, only rarely—is self-evident to him. Nonetheless, they regularly establish a significant *tension* vis-à-vis empirical reality, he maintains. They can and do guide action under certain facilitating circumstances, he is convinced. Hence, they must not be eliminated from sociology's conceptual capital. See, for example, 1946c, p. 324; 1946e, p. 290; see this text, pp. 84–91 and Kalberg 2012, pp. 43–72.

12. Their strengthening today as, for example, "business ethics" and "civic responsibility," is central to the agenda of the Communitarian school. See note 16 below.

13. To the extent that practical-ethical action expands diffusely, many of the "policing" tasks of the state are reduced. *This* manner of confronting and restraining interest-oriented activities results in a more benign, yet more effective, mode of "policing" than that undertaken by the distant and impersonal state and court system (indeed, if to reach the same level of community building, the state would have to assume near totalitarian comprehensiveness). Furthermore, to the degree that civic associations are numerous and permeate widely, a hostility toward the state crystallizes—for it appears to the same

extent to be lacking clear "domestic tranquility" functions and hence less legitimate.

14. This expression will henceforth be used synonymously with "practical-ethical" individualism.

15. Egalitarianism without activity-oriented individualism would imply a massive conformity scarcely imaginable to Americans today. Tocqueville's deep fear of egalitarianism—as leading to a "tyranny of the majority"—is grounded in his neglect of this civic individualism. See Chapter 7.

16. Weber would argue that crisis commentators neglect the significant ways in which the practical-ethical action of disciplined individuals operates in such a symbiotic dualism with (rather than blatant antagonism to) orientations to the civic arena. In other words, these commentators fail to acknowledge the indispensable interlocking and mutually rejuvenating *double axes*—an ethical individualism *oriented to* the civic sphere—at the core of the American political culture's uniqueness. This unsettled dualism not only overtly creates energy, but also sustains an intensely *moral* ingredient, one manifest throughout American history both in the form of social reform movements (for example, Abolitionism, the Women's Suffrage movement, and the Civil Rights movement) and a missionary foreign policy. See Chapters 5 and 6.

CHAPTER FOUR

The Political Culture of the Late Nineteenth and Early Twentieth Centuries

The Strong Individual–Small State Constellation

In countries with old civilizations, matters are much more complicated. For there the struggle between the power of historical notions and the pressure of capitalist interests summon certain social forces to battle as adversaries of bourgeois capitalism. In the United States such forces were partly unknown.

—Weber 2005, pp. 142–143

In [European] countries, where a rural community, aristocratically differentiated, exists, a complex of social and political problems arises. An American finds it difficult to understand the importance of agrarian questions on the European continent, especially in Germany, even in German politics. He will arrive at entirely wrong conclusions if he does not keep before his eyes these great complexes. A peculiar combination of motives is effective in these old countries and explains the deviation of European from American conditions.

—Weber 2005, p. 144

THE PURITAN SECTS remained influential even as industrialization and urbanization unfolded in the latter decades of the nineteenth century. As discussed in the previous chapter, manifest in secular form as practical-ethical action, their ethos now became carried and cultivated by families, neighborhoods, schools, social clubs, and civic groups generally. Constituted as an activity-oriented and self-reliant individualism, it was characterized by resoluteness and a robust optimism regarding the capacity of persons to challenge traditions, shape their own destinies, confront social problems, and contribute to the fulfillment of the civic realm's ideals. It existed, in Weber's terms, "in the world" as a constituent aspect of the American political culture's spirit of democracy—namely, as a civic-oriented individualism. Significant developments throughout the nineteenth century bolstered and sustained this stalwart individualism. All favored a "small state."[1]

This chapter explores this strong individualism–small state constellation. It first examines the American view of the state and then offers comparisons and contrasts to industrializing Germany of the late nineteenth century. However, rather than seeking to offer an in-depth treatment of German political culture, the focus remains on the American case. Heuristic purposes alone determine this turn to Germany: to isolate further central aspects of the political culture of the United States and its spirit of democracy. The concluding section reviews major features of the stalwart individual–small state constellation.[2]

The View of the State in Industrializing America

This nation defined the state in a singular manner. The original immigrants arrived on American shores, hoping to exercise a right to religious expression free from state intervention. Indeed, Puritanism mistrusted fundamentally all secular authority, for its orientation contradicted the ascetic believer's conviction that all energy and activity must be focused exclusively on God, *His* Laws, and the construction of His Kingdom on earth.[3] Hence, the state was perceived with suspicion and as properly empowered to exercise only minimal functions. At the core of the new nation's raison d'être stood the personal liberties guaranteed by the Constitution and Bill of Rights.

An ethos of self-reliance and a firm belief in the individual's capacity to overcome difficult circumstances were grounded in seventeenth-century Puritanism and widespread. The Founding Fathers insisted that the state should ensure the unhindered unfolding of individual rights and societal developments by protecting free debate and an open exchange of views. The just and good society would evolve if the government avoided attempts to guide the lives of citizens and to direct social and economic change, early Americans were convinced. This heritage, as well as Jeffersonian Republicanism, the winning of the West, Horatio Alger "rags to riches" dreams, and the strong reception in the nineteenth century of Classical Liberalism and Social Darwinism, all placed the activity-oriented and "capable" individual on a pedestal. All of these influential currents stood in a relationship of antagonism to the idea of a comprehensive, services-oriented state.[4]

The economic views of Classical Liberalism were formulated most succinctly by Adam Smith (1723–1794) in *The Wealth of Nations* (1981): the "wealth of all" would be best served if individuals were allowed the opportunity to pursue their self-interests free from state interference. This idea, as forcefully articulated in more comprehensive terms by the Utilitarians John Stuart Mill (1806–1873) and Jeremy Bentham (1748–1832), assumed an even broader and principled manifestation: in pursuing their interests generally, individuals would contribute, Mill and Bentham held, to the "common good."

In other words, Utilitarianism banished the notion that the individual's interests stood opposed to those of the larger group. Thus, Classical Liberalism, which became widely influential among American elites, nourished Puritanism's emphasis upon the activity-oriented individual. Even the countervailing response by Transcendentalists in the middle decades of the nineteenth century never proposed an immersion of citizens into a *Gemeinschaft*, or *Volk*; rather, a belief in the individual's capacity to surmount adversity, "to make his way," and to follow an *ethical* course remained dominant. In addition, early and mid-century Jeffersonian and Jacksonian populist beliefs heralded the virtue, wisdom, self-reliance, and good judgment of the "common man" (see Tocqueville 1945, vol. I, pp. 48–60; vol. II, pp. 34–36, 129–136; Lipset 1979; Bellah 1970, pp. 32–35).

The "winning of the frontier" and the accompanying idealization of the "rugged individual" further confirmed the capacity of Americans to *act in the world*. And, as industrialization gathered steam in the 1860s and 1870s, this vigorous individual received extensive praise in penny novels. "Horatio Alger" repeatedly overcame defeat and pulled himself up "by his bootstraps" on the basis of his own talents and energy. At the end of the nineteenth century, energetic individuals empowered to shape their own destinies, to confront all "challenges," to abjure assistance, and to take advantage of putatively bountiful opportunities were extolled by Social Darwinism as those "most fit to survive" (see White 1957; Hofstadter 1955; Konwitz and Kennedy 1960; Sumner 1906).

All of these converging streams affirmed ascetic Protestantism's emphasis on an initiative-taking, capable, and ethical individual. The rapid growth of a largely unrestrained capitalism "from below" in the nineteenth century's latter half, and the severe upheaval that followed, failed to persuade Americans to abandon their self-reliance ethos and scorn for a services-oriented state. Indeed, the Puritanism-based embrace of modern capitalism and entrepreneurship had assisted the birth and growth of a powerful bourgeoisie—a class that directly opposed all aggrandizement of state power and articulated beliefs that praised the beneficent side of capitalism: the striving to fulfill workplace-based goals and the general advantages of competition, individual achievement, and upward mobility. Moreover, this same heritage rejected the notion that an antagonistic relationship existed between the systematic and unregulated pursuit of wealth on the one hand and justice and democracy on the other hand. The "common man's" independence, initiative-taking, and ethical virtues, as well as his good judgment and "can-do" energy, received praise from nearly all quarters.

This activity-oriented and civic individualism contained multiple features at its foundation. As noted, it cultivated an optimistic view regarding the capacity of ethical persons to shape their destinies and to reform their societies. Furthermore, it bestowed the prerequisite self-confidence if viable participation in large-scale political associations is to occur and the defense of threatened civil rights is to be firm. Indeed, owing to enduring legacies of Puritan *asceticism*, this disciplined individualism assessed activity rigorously in terms of its conformity to standards, principles, laws, and ideals. Personal liberties and freedoms of speech, assembly, and the press here acquired the supportive cultural context indispensable to their substantive implementation.[5]

In sum, the self-reliant individualism of seventeenth- and eighteenth-century Puritanism was sustained and rejuvenated in the nineteenth century by a variety of new social and intellectual movements. In this political culture, each nourished and legitimated vigorously a constellation of values antagonistic to government and to secular authority in general. The development of a large state on American soil appeared both unnecessary and undesired.

The boundaries and uniqueness of this stalwart individualism–small state constellation will be more clearly rendered by brief reference to a contrasting case. We now turn to modern Germany during its formative years in the latter decades of the nineteenth century.

Isolating American Uniqueness: The View of the State in Industrializing Germany and the Divergent Location of Practical-Ethical Action

The American definition of the state diverged sharply from the view of the state in modernizing Germany. Capitalism, urbanization, and a thoroughgoing secularization had shattered the old *Gemeinschaft* during this Bismarckian-Wilhelmine era (1871–1917) and caused, Germans frequently believed, unparalleled social and political disorder. A massive "cultural pessimism"—a specter of doom and despair, of malaise and drift—pervaded the German educated classes (*Bildungsbürgertum*; see Ringer 1969; Stern 1965; Mosse 1964; Elias 1981; Kalberg 2012, pp. 227–247). Expectations and hopes congealed around the state, for it was perceived as the only institution in possession of sufficient authority to address these transformations and to prevent social chaos. It became *obligated* to play an active role (see Kocka and Ritter 1974; Plessner 1974; Kocka 1981).

A variety of "protection and care" measures became defined across the political spectrum as both appropriate and necessary. They aimed to assist a population widely understood as structurally disadvantaged and potentially disruptive: unemployment, accident, and health insurance; retirement pensions; wealth redistribution through taxation; and various social welfare benefits. Furthermore, Germans from higher and lower strata alike insisted that the state play a directing role in managing the economy and in promoting a regulated market. This cartel-based economy would, it was believed, effectively confront destabilization dangers.[6] Powerful obstacles in opposition to the unfolding of a manifold state failed to appear, and confidence was lacking in the capacity of individuals, on the basis of their own energy, to adapt to modern capitalism's dislocations (see Holborn 1981; Kocka 1981).

However, this view of the state did not alone define the major axes of the industrializing German political culture. Lutheranism and Catholicism also contributed to the particular *location of practical-ethical* action in German society. Both of these religions, lacking this-worldly asceticism, failed to instill among the faithful an ethos of extreme self-reliance (see Weber 2011c, pp. 104–105; Troeltsch 1960; Mommsen 1974, pp. 81–84; Dillenberger 1961, pp. 363–402). Hence, absent in Germany was a religion-anchored set of values capable of intensely influencing the believer's routine activity—namely, to such a degree that the predominant practical rationalism found in the modernizing political and economy spheres was confronted directly and circumscribed by practical-ethical individualism.

Germany followed a pathway unlike the American: long-standing quasi-feudal and hierarchical conventions and customs penetrated these spheres as urbanization, secularization, and modern capitalism unfolded. Although grounding *patterns* of social activity, and hence protecting against social chaos, these conventions and customs nonetheless restrained practical rationalism's sheer interest-based and calculating relationships in less effective ways than did practical-ethical action. Germans concluded that a circumscription of practical rationalism must occur in a more severe manner, especially in light of long-term and thoroughgoing secularization and widespread social disorder in the 1870s and 1880s.[7] Given the absence of multitudes of *civic* associations capable of serving as powerful social carriers of an expansive civic sphere,[8] a mobilization of the full resources of the state proved both urgent and the single viable alternative.

Accordingly, the state and its laws became the major carriers of social trust and fair play in Germany rather than churches, sects, and civic associations, as in the United States. This configuration was confirmed in Germany by a quasi sanctification of the state that arose on the one hand from the legacies of a highly authoritarian version of

feudalism and on the other hand from Lutheranism's direct legitimation of secular authority (see Troeltsch 1960; Dillenberger 1961, pp.
363–402; Weber 2011c, pp. 103–104).[9] The *ethical* obligations of the
fin de siècle German state involved (a) management and restriction
of the capitalist economy; (b) implementation of an array of social
equity, social welfare, and social cohesion measures in general; (c) the
construction and implementation—through a court system—of a
comprehensive legal code; and (d) guarantees of formal equality before
the law. This state possessed legitimacy on a sustained basis to combat
advanced industrialism's social problems.[10]

Thus, in Germany the state became a central fulcrum and major
point of reference far more than in the industrializing United States.
Two important consequences followed, both of which further assist
our aim of defining the uniqueness of the American political culture
and its spirit of democracy: first, in Germany, practical-ethical action
became more focused around the state and, second, the legitimacy
of the political realm became more closely tied to the state's success
in combating the social disorder and inequities believed to be indigenous to capitalism, secularism, and urbanism. Hence, whereas broad
arrays of civic associations—each articulating ethical ideals in tension
with practical rationalism—composed a *diffuse and extended political
arena* in the American case, the state more so constituted this domain
in industrializing Germany. Political parties and unions, although
significant in scale, failed to compete in this regard with the state's
overwhelming power and authority.

Thus, diverging views of the state and its appropriate responsibilities are apparent in industrializing Germany and the United States.
Heterogeneity is evident despite the structural constraints common to
industrialization and urbanization. Distinct features characterize the
American political culture and spirit of capitalism: an extended civic
sphere, a "small state" and a posture of hostility toward the state, and
a practical-ethical, civic-oriented individualism. Chapters 1, 2, and 3
examined the anchoring of these features in ascetic Protestantism in
the seventeenth and eighteenth centuries and in civic associations in
the nineteenth century.

Albeit in a highly abbreviated manner, the Weber-inspired interpretation presented in this chapter has addressed four themes pivotal in the

American political culture in the late nineteenth and early twentieth centuries: its activist individualism, accentuated civic sphere, unique view of the modern state, and singular location of political-ethical action. In part through a comparison with industrializing Germany, major and distinct *American* contours in respect to each theme have been isolated.

All of these themes will be revisited in the following two chapters in *analytic* discussions of the American political culture's origins, parameters, and oscillations. Chapter 5 commences with an examination of Weber's vision of the future. He queries whether an "iron cage" society is already visible on the horizon. Will the American civic sphere and its spirit of democracy in general, amid large-scale bureaucratization, experience a severe weakening?

Notes

1.   As will become evident, this phrase refers to a fundamental antagonism in the American political culture to a comprehensive, social welfare–oriented state along European lines. "Weak state" is used synonymously.

2.   Compared with earlier chapters and Chapter 5, this chapter constitutes more of a "Weberian interpretation" and "Weberian study"; it is less anchored in an exegesis of Weber's writings.

3.   Puritanism's *asceticism* required, without equivocation, that even secular rulers must be understood (as the devout generally) as "vessels" of God's laws rather than as authorities in possession of an independent legitimation. This wariness vis-à-vis authority is also grounded in the Puritan view that rulers, owing to their possession of great power, are particularly liable to vanity and an exaggeration of their self-worth—both of which, because they contest the believer's appropriate focus on God and His commandments, must be circumscribed. Weber documents this significant aspect of Puritanism on a number of occasions. See this text, pp. 24–25 and Appendix II.

4.   This paragraph is indebted to Bailyn 1967; Dewey 1922, 1989; Konwitz and Kennedy 1960; Lipset 1979.

5.   Just such a legacy of asceticism lies at the foundation of a posture such as that expressed by Thomas Paine during the Revolutionary War: "although I do not agree with what you say, I will defend to the death your right to say it." Even though residuals of this posture can be found empirically in American political (as well as social) life even today (e.g., most notably among supporters of the American Civil Liberties Union, an organization of lawyers dedicated to

defend the rights of individuals regardless of the manner in which they have been infringed), its more widespread manifestations appear in more routinized forms: for example, the respect for law, the punitive (vs. rehabilitative) character of the American criminal justice system (see Savelsberg 1994, 1999; Savelsberg and King 2005), and the "missionary" and "can-do" tenor of its foreign policy (see Kalberg 1991, 2003).

6. Of course, the state was granted a directing role over the economy, owing significantly to the dominant belief that German industrialization must "catch up" with its international competitors, mainly England and the United States. A cartel-based economy, it was widely believed, would be the most efficient means of doing so. See Berghahn 2005.

7. A far greater secularization existed throughout Europe in the nineteenth century than in the United States, as is the case today. See Pew Forum, November 17, 2011: www.pewforum.org.

8. This is not to say that associations (*Vereine*) did not exist in Germany. This view has been appropriately discredited. Rather, *Vereine* were unpolitical (hiking, chess, choral, etc.), and political parties were polarized. Thus, and also as a consequence of the authoritarian character of this protection and care state, a strong civic sphere could not develop.

9. For the contrast to Puritanism, see this text, pp. 24–25.

10. In this sense, laws and statutes of the German state must be understood as the carriers of early-nineteenth-century German Romanticism's ideals of universalism and inclusion (see Brunschwig 1975). That these ideals became socially located in the state rather than in sects and churches would have far-reaching effects on the formation of Germany's political culture in the twentieth century.

CHAPTER FIVE

The Weberian Model

The Dissolution of the American Civic Sphere in the Twentieth Century

> [Democracy and freedom] ... are [possible], in fact, only where, over a period of time, they are supported by the resolute *will* of a nation not to allow itself to be led like a flock of sheep.
>
> —*Weber 1978, p. 282; emphasis in original*

ORIGINATING IN THE agrarian and religious landscapes of the seventeenth and eighteenth centuries, the American civic sphere confronted severe challenges in the nineteenth and twentieth centuries, Max Weber holds. Deeply anchored in ascetic Protestantism, would this sphere, and the American spirit of democracy in general, retain an independent influence? Urbanization, industrialization, and modern capitalism implied a massive societal metamorphosis.

American society, rendered conducive to the values of an expanding entrepreneurial class by ascetic Protestantism, became permeated by the orientation of action to competition, achievement, hard work, self-reliance, upward mobility, an optimistic frame of mind in respect to the individual's ability, and an energetic approach to problems and tasks. By the 1870s, heroes in Horatio Alger's mold, severed from binding tradition and exclusively reliant on their own talent, energy, and will, climbed from rags to riches. Standing alone, the individual became in major circles respected, worthy of praise, and placed on a pedestal. Weber queried whether the symbiotic dualism of the nineteenth century—the synthesis of a practical-ethical individualism with a strong civic sphere—would remain in place in the twentieth century. Or would a rejuvenated practical rationalism banish this civic-oriented individualism? Would innumerable civic associations continue to permeate the American political culture and support a community-building infrastructure to such a degree that a circumscription of sandpile atomization would occur? Even though still substantially nourished at the end of the nineteenth century by churches and civic associations, great social transformations, Weber argues, severely challenged the civic realm's foundations—and hence its spirit of democracy.

Of course, he viewed corruption and a "spoils system" as widespread in the American society of the late nineteenth and early twentieth centuries. Moreover, he saw that power and crass calculation frequently prevailed over the call to ideals. Indeed, Weber perceived the corrupt politics of city machines as unusually pervasive and ethical action in reference to a civic ethos as the exception (1946b, pp. 108–110; 1968, p. 1401; 1978, pp. 281–282). It appeared significantly weakened by practical rationalism.

The *possible fates* of a thick American civic sphere in the rapidly changing twentieth and twenty-first centuries must now be addressed. Weber's concepts and analytic framework continue to accompany and guide our analysis of the American political culture even as we now shift away from the distant past and toward the more immediate past and the present. We must first examine his general views on the twentieth century. Was an "iron cage" autocracy on the horizon?

The Modern World: An Iron Cage?[1]

Weber viewed the coming of industrial capitalism with trepidation and foreboding. Indeed, at times he depicts the modern era as a cold and impersonal "iron cage" (*stahlhartes Gehäuse*). How does he define this phrase? Does this metaphor accurately capture his view of the modern American political culture? Does it imply the suffocation of its spirit of democracy?

These queries guide this chapter. It first examines Weber's analysis of the weakening in our own epoch of the American civic sphere. The new symbiotic dualism in this nation's political culture, as discussed in Chapter 3, is revisited. Its fragility, in light of twentieth-century structural transformations, is explored.

A *Weberian model* is then reconstructed. Its three sub-constructs investigate the "privatization of work," the "Europeanization" of American society, and the "power of material goods." All evidence of an expansion of *practical rationalism* to such an extent that Weber sees the American civic sphere as distinctly endangered. Its survival appeared to him unlikely.

He argued in *The Protestant Ethic* that Puritan asceticism involved an unusually methodical orientation toward work. As it spread widely across the American landscape in the nineteenth century, this ethos, as noted in Chapter 3, lost its religious foundations. Yet its secular heir, in the form of a vocational calling (*Beruf*), remained: a *spirit* of capitalism (see Appendix II). It assisted at the birth of an industrial and highly organized form of capitalism.

However, earlier linked intricately to the motivation to work methodically, *values* are no longer crucial to, or cultivated in, "modern industrial labor," Weber contends—even though work in the twentieth century has been placed upon a pedestal: "The idea of an 'obligation to search for and then accept a vocational calling' now wanders around in our lives as the ghost of past religious beliefs" (2011c, p. 177). Those born today into this "modern economic order" are no longer motivated to work systematically on the basis of a calling; rather, "this economy … bound to the technical and economic conditions of mechanized, machine-based production" (2011c, p. 178) coerces us to do so in order to survive. "Overwhelming force" now characterizes capitalism and a mighty structure founded in a "formal rationality" of technical, administrative, and market contingencies determines our lives. This "mechanical foundation" anchors modern capitalism now and encompasses our workplace activity (2011c, pp. 177–178). Moreover, Weber emphasizes that the advance of modern capitalism in the West occurred parallel to the development of a specific organization supremely adapted to its functioning. It affirms an indispensable value: technically superior administration.

> The bureaucratic organization, with its specialization of trained skills, its delineation of competencies, its rules and hierarchical relations of obedience ... is ... in the process of erecting a cage of bondage which persons—lacking all powers of resistance—will perhaps one day be forced to inhabit, as the fellahs of ancient Egypt. This *might happen if a purely technical value—a rational civil service administration and distribution of welfare benefits— becomes viewed as the ultimate and single value in reference to which the organization of all affairs ought to be decided.* The bureaucracy achieves this result much better than any other structure of domination. (1968, p. 1402; translation altered, emphasis in original)

In this steel-hard casing, the omnipresence of bureaucracies calls forth a caste of functionaries and civil servants. "A fettering [of] every individual to his job ... his class ... and maybe to his occupation" occurs. Opportunities for the development of genuine entrepreneurs and political leaders vanish in this closed and rigidly stratified society "as austerely rational as a machine." Wherever the "inescapable power" of the bureaucracy's functionaries reigns, a "pacifism of social impotence," a loss of all societal dynamism, and a thorough societal stagnation result (1968, pp. 1402–1403; see also Weber 1978, pp. 281–283).

Devoid of brotherhood, compassion, and heroic ethical action, this inflexible "cosmos" becomes more and more dominated by the impersonal and cautious values of the functionary on the one hand—duty, punctuality, reliability, and respect for the organization's hierarchy— and practical rationalism's calculations of interests and advantage on the other hand. A retreat into the private realm of intimacy, where emotion and person-oriented values still pulsate, and the *cultivation* of this private realm, are viewed as the single means of survival with a measure of dignity in tact. "Home and hearth" become the refuge; here alone warmth and deep bonds are found. All civic virtues and public ethics are absent from this "impersonal mechanism," and most values overarching the private domain exist as moribund legacies from earlier, mainly religion-saturated, epochs. They are now threatened with extinction by the mighty, inexorable expansion of calculation, manipulation, and practical rationality generally (Weber 2011c, pp. 177–178; 2005, pp. 270–271, 339).

Innumerable commentators to this day have comprehended this portrait as Weber's actual characterization of our times; others have maintained that he viewed this bleak scenario as on the distant horizon. In both cases, Weber is portrayed as a dour and haunted figure, fatalistic and despairing, yet also heroic and stoical—a brooding giant who carried the burdens of the present and future upon his broad shoulders.

It must be acknowledged that his view of the modern era was a distant cry from that of contemporary Anglo-Saxon theorists who hailed the coming of the industrial age as "progress," a new advance of civilization, and a further stage in the triumphant evolution of mankind. Weber also clearly parted ways with all "theorists of democracy," who discovered in the industrialized society a broad and deep *civic* realm of open participation, personal liberties, and public ideals and ethics. Had he still been writing in the 1950s, he would have sharply disagreed with the Modernization theorists, all of whom asserted (in one way or another) that capitalism itself calls forth democracy and that democracy's advance proceeds roughly parallel with the march of industrialism (see Parsons 1966, 1971, 2007).

Nonetheless, the iron cage metaphor fails to encapsulate Weber's complex view of the present and the future. First, rather than a reality, or even a short-term scenario, this steel-hard casing constituted to him a nightmare vision that *might* be on our horizon. The subjunctive case, qualifying expressions, and multiple preconditions are almost always attached to his usage of this phrase (see 1968, pp. 559–560, 960–961, 991, 1403–1404; Mommsen 1974, pp. 86–87).

Second, in central ways Weber *welcomed* the modern world—in particular the freedoms and rights it bestowed upon individuals and the very notion of the autonomous individual—and scorned the past, as well as the naive romanticism of most of his colleagues: "After all, it is a gross deception to believe that without the achievements of the age of the 'Rights of Man,' any one of us (including the most conservative) can go on living his life" (1968, p. 1403).[2] He spoke and wrote tirelessly in support of strong and contending political parties, a constitutional division of powers, an "ethic of responsibility" for politicians, constitutional guarantees of civil liberties, and an extension of suffrage (see 1968, p. 1462; 1946b, pp. 115–127). Furthermore, he argued vehemently that democracy would be possible only where a strong parliament existed, which he saw as a training ground for the political leaders of the "plebiscitary leadership democracy" he advanced (1968, pp. 1409–1414; Mommsen 1974). Finally, he sought to erect various mechanisms that would sustain the pluralistic and competing groups he saw as capable of checking the power of bureaucracies, for "we 'individualist' and party member partisans of 'democratic' institutions … are swimming 'against the tide' of material constellations" (1978, p. 282; see pp. 281–282).

Rather than the fatalism and despair so prominent among his contemporaries in Germany, particularly Nietzsche and Georg Simmel, skepticism mixed with appreciation characterizes Weber's position. He believed that industrial societies, *if dynamic*, offered an opportunity for the development of the autonomous individual guided by *ethical* values (Weber 1946b, pp. 115–127; 1968, pp. 960–961, 979–980, 1207–1210; 1978, p. 282; see Löwith 1970; Mommsen 1974, pp. 86–87, 93–95; Kalberg 2011b).

Thirdly, the common portrayal of Weber as a sociologist who saw the present and future as an iron cage is derived largely from his political and social-philosophical essays rather than from his sociological writings.[3] If extracted from his comparative-historical texts, his view regarding industrial and urban societies is both *more dynamic* and *more differentiated* than the steel-hard casing metaphor suggests. They are best conceptualized, he contends, as mixtures—even *dynamic* mixtures—of the past and the present. Indeed, Weber's mode of analysis advocates an examination of each particular country and an assessment of its *uniqueness* (see Kalberg 1994, pp. 81–84). His focus remains on *cases* rather than putatively global, irreversible, and monolithic developments (see Chapter 7, pp. 106–109).

Although both Germany and the United States, for example, were quite advanced industrial societies at the end of the nineteenth century, they were separated by many significant differences.[4] A strong social welfare state prevailed in Germany, as well as a powerful elite of state civil servants, an authoritarian centralization of power, an ineffective and weak parliament, a passive citizenry "governed like sheep," a state church highly supportive of state authority, hierarchical social conventions, industrialization directed "from above" by the state, and a formal-rational—Continental—legal system anchored exclusively in a constitution (Weber 1968, pp. 1381–1469; Kalberg 2003; 2012, pp. 227–248). On the other hand, in the United States a quite different configuration became prominent: a decentralized and "weak state," an activist citizenry and ubiquitous civic associations, a separation of church and state, antiauthoritarian religious institutions, industrialization "from below," a legal system (although based in a constitution) strongly indebted to the emphasis in English Common Law on precedent, and comparatively egalitarian social customs (see Weber 1988, pp. 438–448; 1946d; 1968, pp. 1197–1210). Finally, the social prestige of civil servants, so high in Germany and so central to the iron cage model, is seen to be unusually low:

> Usually the social esteem of the officials is especially low where the demand for expert administration and the hold of status conventions are weak. This is often the case in new settlements by virtue of the great economic opportunities and the great instability of their social stratification: witness the United States. (1968, p. 960)

Thus, again, the common depiction of Weber as upholding a monolithic—and iron cage—vision of the modern epoch must be rejected. His sociological writings maintain that the political culture of each industrial nation is distinct unto itself. Even in respect to "bureaucratization," he insists on case-specific contextualization.

> One must in every individual historical case analyze the special direction in which bureaucratization develops. For this reason, it must remain an open question whether the *power* of bureaucracy is, without exception, increasing in the modern states in which it is spreading.... Thus whether the power of bureaucracy as such increases cannot be decided *a priori*. (1968, p. 1991; translation altered)

In sum, the iron cage metaphor must be understood as of limited usefulness for a review and discussion of the American political culture and its spirit of democracy today. Weber's analysis of its underlying contours, as examined in Chapters 1 through 4, delineated a highly unique configuration. Further central questions must now be pursued. How did the transformation from an agrarian, deeply Puritan, and rural society to an industrial, urban, and more secular nation in the twentieth century alter this political culture? Weber queries whether, for example, the thick civic sphere, so deeply anchored in American religious history, will retain a significant sociological impact.

The Weberian Model: The Dissolution of the Civic Sphere

A reconstructed "Weberian model" identifies a multitude of threats to the civic arena's viability and to practical-ethical action in general. It summarizes the several ways in which Weber viewed the weakening and dissolution of the American civic realm. Pivotal here are three sub-constructs that chart important developments: "the privatization of work," "the power of goods," and the "Europeanization" models. All map the magnitude of the societal metamorphosis, demarcate central features of the American political culture, and formulate hypotheses regarding challenges to the civic arena.[5] Brief scrutiny of each must suffice.

The Privatization of Work and the Expansion of Practical Rationalism

According to this sub-model, both the early Puritan sanctification of work and the nineteenth century's practical-ethical action grounded in civic associations had faded significantly by the beginning of the twentieth century. A values-based individualism had become routinized back to an interest-based individualism. This construct hypothesizes that a depletion and circumscription of the civic arena followed. A vicious cycle ensued. A brief review of each stage in this centuries-transcending process is necessary.

The aim in the Colonial era to build on earth God's Kingdom, although weakened with the waning of Puritan asceticism, endured in secularized form, this model postulates: Americans sought to establish the *just society* in the latter eighteenth century and throughout the nineteenth century. Unsurprisingly in light of this religious heritage, work, investment, and community service became viewed as the central means toward this end. Thus, a nurturing of the earlier symbiotic dualism between the construction of God's just community and world-mastery individualism occurred, albeit increasingly—as practical-ethical action replaced world-mastery individualism—in secularized manifestations. However, as the nineteenth century drew to a close, the civic sphere commenced again on a pathway of decline. Its capacity *to direct* the activity of broad cross sections of the American population weakened amid expanding industrialism and urbanism. An individualism anchored in practical-rationalism now gained traction.

In this new society neither Benjamin Franklin's spirit of capitalism nor the Puritans' Protestant ethic endowed methodical work with subjective meaning (Weber 2011c, pp. 177–178). As the historical journey distinguished by asceticism's prodigious sanctification of work drew to a close, labor became simply a utilitarian activity—namely, an activity oriented mainly to the individual's private concerns. Now decoupled from the religion sphere and routinized back to its practical-rational form, work more and more exclusively served the pragmatic interests of individuals.

The full *privatization* dominant at the final stage of this monumental journey is captured by this "privatization of work" sub-construct. It also depicts the social context that, according to Weber, influenced this development: modern capitalism's coercive aspects and practical rationalism. Whether employees or entrepreneurs, those "born into this powerful cosmos" are forced to adapt to market-based laws and the impersonal exchange of goods. Once "in the saddle," "victorious capitalism's" workplace tempo, rather than an orientation of citizens to the supernatural realm or to the civic sphere, imposes on all an organized mode of life. The survival of businesses, as well as the individual's capacity to earn a livelihood, requires nothing less, for this "grinding mechanism" is characterized by an "inescapable network of pragmatic necessities." According to this sub-construct, the modern era's foundation is not "spiritual" but "mechanical." In one of his most famous passages, Weber tersely captures this significant transformation at the level of subjective meaning and motives: "The Puritan *wanted* to be a person with a vocational calling; we *must* be" (2011c, p. 177, see pp. 177–178; 2011b, pp. 269–271; see Appendix II).

Of central significance for the fate of the civic arena, work in this sub-construct is eviscerated of its prior religious and civic underpinnings, as well as all community-building and integrative capacities—even though it remains at the center of daily life. Hence, this sub-model hypothesizes a massive shift away from both the Puritan values indigenous to world-mastery individualism and even from the nineteenth century's symbiotic dualism, and toward unsanctified labor and an expanding practical-rational individualism. Increasingly, the practical-ethical action that nourished the civic realm is pushed to the margins; the patterned orientation of citizen action to the civic arena's ideals reaches its final stage. This activity becomes redefined as a hobby endeavor and relocated within the arena of leisure. The American spirit of democracy soon vanishes.

The Circumscription of the Civic Sphere by "Europeanization"

Weber's second sub-construct postulates a gradual *Europeanization* of American political culture.[6] It views large-scale organizations as inherent to industrial societies and sees bureaucratization as whittling away and constricting the civic arena. Again, the spirit of democracy is directly threatened.

The constraints accompanying industrialization render this alteration likely, this sub-model hypothesizes. An increase in the prestige and authority of civil servants and managers occurs, Weber contends. Their specialized knowledge of the workings of the state and the economy underpin these developments, and this aggrandizement of bureaucracies is accompanied by a diminution of authority by elected politicians over policy-making decisions. With ever-widening bureaucratization, a civic realm dominated by contending political parties, open debate, pluralistic and competing values, and freedom of ideas undergoes contraction, this sub-construct postulates. As conflict becomes tame and then quiescent, civic ideals—no longer rejuvenated by the widespread controversies that appear wherever groups compete vigorously—fade as well (1968, pp. 1396–1405; 1978, pp. 281–282; 1971b).

A "societal ossification" follows, according to this sub-model, intensified by ever greater class stratification and restricted occupational and social mobility. The survival of practical-ethical action becomes questionable—all the more as the prestige and authority of functionaries increase. A rigid, inward-looking, and stagnant society, dominated by risk-averse, security-seeking, and cautious managers, appears. The civic arena, as well as all residuals of the sect spirit's community-building energy, is pushed to the margins. Simultaneously, the bureaucracy's *formal* rationality, in light of its orientation to procedures, statutes, codes, and written regulations, confronts and weakens further legacies of the world-mastery and practical-ethical forms of individualism rooted in values, this sub-construct holds. Hence, survival of the nineteenth century's symbiotic dualism—an interweaving of practical-ethical individualism with the civic sphere—is unlikely. Circumscription of the civic realm's independence and a severe weakening of its expansive thrust follow (Weber 2005, pp. 255–272).[7] The American spirit of democracy is extinguished.

The Circumscription of the Civic Sphere by the "Power of Material Goods"

A significant development in more recent decades—the expansion of the "power of material goods"—affirms the individual untamed by values and stands in a relationship of antagonism to a vibrant civic realm. A further Weberian sub-model captures this transformation of the American political culture and its outcome: an expansion of practical rationalism.

Under "victorious capitalism," the power of goods acquires a firm grip over persons, this sub-construct postulates. Seventeenth- and eighteenth-century Puritans, living *in this* world but oriented to the *next* world, could easily resist attractive products—like "a lightweight coat that one can throw off at any time." However, in the twentieth century the power of these goods increased massively; they became "a steel-hard casing" (2011c, pp. 163–164, 176–178).

Material goods now acquire, this sub-model hypothesizes, "an increasing and, in the end, inescapable power over people—as never before in history" (2011c, p. 178). An omnipresent and intense consumer culture develops parallel with the onset of prosperity. Alluring products must be possessed. Moreover, the striving for their acquisition has assumed a new intensity and become a vigorous "pursuit of gain in the United States," this sub-construct holds, displacing the vocational calling's spirit of asceticism. This quest in the twentieth century resembles the "character of a sports event": "purely competitive passions" now reign (2011c, p. 178; see Bell 1996).

Thus, as industrialism rapidly spreads, individualism in America became directed less and less to a constellation of civic values and more and more to material prosperity. An intensity unrivaled in other postindustrial nations is apparent. Thoroughly interwoven with and invigorated by the civic realm in the nineteenth century, this individualism in the twentieth century became severed from this guiding force to a significant degree. It is today systematically courted and cultivated by Madison Avenue executives with social science degrees. A public sphere now penetrated widely by consumer products and images renders civic ideals narrower in scope. Advertisements offer friendliness, comfort, excitation, images of romance, and hope for the individual's prosperity.

This new American political culture is distinct in a further manner. Whereas the symbiotic dualism of the nineteenth century implied a strong civic component that held in check a decline of task-oriented, practical-ethical individualism into practical-rational individualism, the recent dualism places very different barriers against interest-based orientations. Because all sustained contributions to community improvement, as well as all attempts to overcome evil on behalf of praise for God's greater glory, are enfeebled, the civic arena loses its capacity to pull and direct individualism; rather, both subtle and overt pressures to conform to the fashionable, the hot, and the trendy now do so. Whereas the practical-ethical individualism–civic sphere dualism of the nineteenth century invoked a mutually sustaining dynamism that invigorated *both* components of the American spirit of democracy, the individualism-consumer dualism today pursues a different agenda:

instead of erecting obstacles against the individual's exclusive orientation to material prosperity, a close alignment of this orientation with
the consumer culture is apparent.

The consequence is evident according to this sub-model: a ubiquitous consumerist ethos further invigorates practical-rational individualism. An acceleration of the civic realm's porousness follows.
Its independence wanes, as well as all residuals of practical-ethical
action. Again, a vicious cycle ensues. Although perhaps not immediately apparent, the long-term outcome is clear: the practical-ethical
individualism–civic arena symbiotic dualism is weakened, societal
dynamism and openness become constricted, and an unequivocal
drift toward greater social conformism occurs.[8] The American spirit
of democracy is unable to endure in this context.

These three sub-constructs depict *Weber's conceptualizations* of the
American civic sphere in the twentieth century. Taken together, they
constitute *the Weberian model*—namely, a construct that defines possible future parameters of the American political culture and its spirit
of democracy according, on the one hand, to the analytic framework
and rich set of concepts summarized in Chapters 1 through 4 of this
work and, on the other hand, to a variety of Weber's writings.

The privatization of work, the power of material goods, and Europeanization models all postulate the civic sphere's dissolution: all significantly challenge practical-ethical individualism and hence also the
continued viability of the civic arena. Weber cautions that contributions
to the stable functioning of American democracy by world-mastery and
practical-ethical individualism have occurred *only* as a consequence of
their firm orientations to a substantive civic realm. Again, individualism
here must be described as a *civic individualism*. Conversely, as discussed,
owing to its utilitarian character, practical-rational individualism proves
incapable of offering sustenance to the civic sphere.

Weber's analysis never "guarantees" that a values-based individualism will either arise and prove victorious vis-à-vis a practical-rational
individualism *or* become oriented to civic sphere ideals to a binding
degree. *Activity consistent* with these ideals is grounded in a *patterned*
way—and sustained—only if a practical-ethical individualism becomes
manifest. Under conditions of urbanization, advanced industrialism,

postindustrialism, and vast consumerism, the likelihood increases that this individualism will wither and become transformed into a practical-rational individualism directed exclusively to self-interests and emotional desires. This metamorphosis appears all the more plausible wherever the occupational and leisure spheres offer manifold rewards that appeal directly to the fulfillment of these interests and desires (see Chapter 6).

A *cultivation* of individualism then occurs: its activities are neither restrained by, nor channeled toward, a civic sphere. In the context of the twenty-first century, all movement in this direction would seem to be driven by causes that must be deemed, from the point of view of Weber's sociology, comparatively weak: legacies from the past and verbal admonitions by "persons of goodwill." A values-based individualism then, in all likelihood, fails to compete with—let alone banish—practical rationalism's utilitarianism. Long threatened, the symbiotic dualism of the nineteenth century proves incapable of rejuvenation and restoration in the twentieth and twenty-first centuries. The spirit of American democracy contracts.

Three further constructs must now be formulated. Indebted also to Weber's concepts and analytic framework, each *expands on* the Weberian model's analytical framework. They offer further conceptual tools that assist demarcation of the American political culture today and, in particular, the contours and transformations of its civic sphere. They also formulate hypotheses that speak to recent empirical research. The next chapter reconstructs these "complementary" models.

Notes

1. The high visibility of this phrase requires that it be retained for now. "Steel-hard casing" is a more accurate rendering and is used here synonymously. See this text, pp. 19–20 and the Glossary.
2. Weber here refers to the French Enlightenment.
3. The prominent exception is the passage at the end of *PE* (2011c, p. 177).
4. On this theme, see the previous chapter.
5. Thus, the conceptual yield of Weber's analysis is stressed in this chapter rather than its empirical accuracy. This aspect—building concepts

and hypotheses—of Weber's sociology will be emphasized here. Hence, this chapter seeks to use Weber's concepts and analytic framework: it offers a purely *analytical* consideration that charts the full spectrum in reference to which the civic sphere's (according to Weber) movements across the American political culture occur. According to his methodology, such "clear conceptualization," model building, and hypothesis formation must always constitute the *first* step in the research process—that is, a stage prior to commencement of the empirical investigation (see Weber 1949, pp. 90–104).

    6. This is Weber's term. See 2011d, pp. 210, 216.

    7. Again, the "Weberian sub-models" are constructed here as hypothesis-forming aids for research rather than as constructs designed to capture empirical reality. Interpreters have generally comprehended Weber's "Europeanization thesis" as an empirical development and offered trenchant criticisms. See Mommsen 1974, 1998, 2000; Roth 1985, 2005a, 2005b.

    8. Although Weber only vaguely foresaw this metamorphosis (see 2011c, pp. 177–178), he would not have been surprised at this paradoxical turn in which a single factor originating from an orientation to transcendent commandments and religious values—a world-mastery individualism—in a later historical epoch subverted its indispensable sustaining counterpart: substantial and demarcated civic sphere ideals. He had discovered throughout the histories of the East and West such ironic twists and unforeseen consequences of this order of historical magnitude. They stand at the very foundation of his comparative-historical sociology. See Kalberg 1994; 2012, pp. 43–139, 205–224.

CHAPTER SIX

Complementary Models

Expanding the Weberian Model

> After all, it is a gross self-deception to believe that without the achievements of the age of the Rights of Man any one of us, including the most conservative, can go on living his life.
>
> —*Weber 1968, p. 1403*

> Policy-making is not a technical affair, and hence not the business of the professional civil servant.
>
> —*Weber 1968, p. 1419*

THE WEBERIAN MODEL of the twentieth-century American political culture reconstructed in Chapter 5 postulates a severe weakening, and even dissolution, of the civic sphere and, hence, of the American spirit of democracy. However, and although it includes differentiated sub-constructs, this model depicts only one of several possible outcomes. Weber's analytic treatise, *Economy and Society*, offers an additional array of salient concepts and hypotheses. When juxtaposed, they formulate a "complementary" construct. It captures this political culture's significant further features, tensions, dynamics, and developmental pathways. In doing so, this model extends the conceptual reach of the Weberian model.

The complementary construct hypothesizes a more widespread influence for the civic sphere. It formulates three sub-models for the

American political culture: the "generalization," "professional associations," and "conflict" constructs. Each charts a *possible* empirical pathway; all prove indispensable for the further comprehension of the civic sphere's distinct contours and transformations today. In combination, they capture its movements across a spectrum from more thick, expansive, and independent manifestations to more porous, circumscribed, and dependent forms. Together, the complementary and Weberian models constitute a *Weberian analysis* that demarcates the American political culture's full spectrum and its present-day spirit of democracy.[1]

The Generalization Model: The Civic Sphere's Longevity

Compared with the Weberian model, the generalization sub-construct anchors the opposite end of the spectrum. At its foundation stands a core assumption of Weber's sociology: the past never fades away as a consequence of structural changes; rather, it endures to a significant extent into the present.

According to this sub-model, the practical-ethical individualism of the nineteenth century retains its civic orientation over a longer period. In addition, the focus of this individualism on work endures and aggressively sustains a community-building element. A notion of "service to a community" is prolonged, and the values-based *symbiotic* dualism between practical-ethical activity and the civic sphere remains vibrant. Hence, a thick civic realm maintains its expansiveness and independence. The spirit of American democracy endures.

An empirically viable civic individualism here defends its boundaries against practical rationalism, Europeanization, and the power of goods. By injecting a pluralistic dynamism, the sheer multitude and wide dispersion of civic associations resist societal stagnation. Moreover, this broad pluralism of groups independently cultivates civic arena values and a practical-ethical individualism. Hence, the influence of civic associations survives and retains its generalized influence across various sectors of American society. The policy-making arena continues to be rooted in electoral politics and a strong legislative branch.

Wherever these carrier groups acquire authority, status, and power vis-à-vis opposing groups, the civic realm retains its thick consistency and independence, this model postulates. Rather than expanding exclusively into the arenas of work or politics, it spreads generally across the breadth of the American landscape: practical-ethical action—a civic individualism—extends into families, neighborhoods, schools, charity groups, foundations, volunteer groups, universities, the military, and other mainstream organizations and institutions.

As discussed in Chapter 5, the Weberian model's secularism weakened both the civic sphere *and* practical-ethical individualism—indeed it postulated a severe weakening, and even dissolution, of the civic realm. However, according to the generalization construct, work retains its sanctified—or quasi-sanctified—element far longer. Thus, all of these organizations and institutions continue to transmit a community-building energy.

In sum, despite nineteenth- and twentieth-century structural transformations of a prodigious degree, the generalization model hypothesizes that the civic sphere substantially maintains its earlier intensity and influence.[2] In direct contrast to the Weberian construct, a thick and independent civic arena is sustained.[3] This model captures significant features of American society today.

A brief discussion of the manner in which "moral values" played a significant role in the 2004 election campaign will demonstrate its salience. Twenty-two percent of American voters declared moral values the "most important issue" in the election. Twenty percent of the electorate viewed the economy, 19 percent terror, and 15 percent Iraq as "most important." What are "moral values," and why were they more important than the war in Iraq? The generalization model clarifies their relevance. The application of this construct to an analysis of this election illustrates its explanatory power. It also indicates the present-day significance of the American spirit of democracy.

The Role of Moral Values in the 2004 Presidential Election: An Application of the Generalization Model

As discussed previously, practical-ethical individualism came to be uniquely located in the United States in civic associations in the nineteenth century (see Chapter 3). These ubiquitous organizations carried constellations of values diffusely into activities pursued in every corner of American society. In the process, they cultivated, and rejuvenated, a broad-ranging, value-anchored civic sphere. Whether manifest as "public ethics" or "moral values," this arena constituted a realm of activity oriented to ethical ideals—hence activity in opposition to all routinization of action in the direction of utilitarian and practical-rational calculations. How did these "moral values" become overt and influential during the 2004 presidential election? This explanation is now familiar to us.

Echoes and legacies of the moral rigor typical in devout seventeenth- and eighteenth-century communities endured, passed across the generations in tempered and secular forms by carrier groups: families, schools, neighborhoods, workplace organizations, and varieties of civic associations. Although altered further by the social transformations accompanying twentieth-century urbanization and industrialization, these social carriers ensured that a strictness in respect to ideal behavior would be perpetually rejuvenated. Regular appeals to "community standards" and their enforcement agencies cultivated an awareness of, and sensitivity to, questions of ethical conduct. Recognizable *standards* for proper conduct remained, and applied to both business and political figures. Although secular, a broad-ranging rejuvenation of the "sect legacy" occurred periodically in this manner.[4] Hence, throughout the twentieth century, legacies of Protestant asceticism's self-reliance ethos, rigorous disciplining of the believer's entire conduct of life, and "respectable demeanor" could be found, even if uninfluenced by sincere belief and monitoring congregations. Strong residuals of past religious and quasi-religious norms became apparent in all definitions of acceptable behavior.

The character of persons who seek to lead their communities, in whatever domain of life, even today must exhibit a certain "upright" quality. A demeanor that outwardly demonstrates moral rigor, honesty, and trustworthiness must be manifest, for this conduct testifies—it is widely perceived—to a capacity to act consistently in reference to a set of firm values. Continuity of behavior over the course of adulthood is viewed as proving the presence of a firm moral compass. Clarity of purpose and a clear-cut resolve is equated with a straightforward mode of decision making, as well as candor, both with one's God and in human relationships. Exemplary moral character is also "proven" through adherence to a conventional mode of life and the exemplary personal situation (the impeccable past, the dignified wife, the well-behaved and respectful children, the long-term marriage).

Residual components of ascetic Protestantism—a firm resolve in respect to values and standards, consistency over the long term, "good moral character," and so on—were unusually manifest in the 2004 campaign. Indeed, the extreme salience of moral values in this election becomes plausible, especially to the foreign observer, only if the ascetic Protestant imprint on the political culture of the United States is acknowledged. The degree of intensity assumed by moral issues can be comprehended only by reference to a deeply historical, and uniquely American, dynamic. Whether prayer in the public schools should be permitted constituted a major electoral topic in many regions; deep concerns were evident throughout the nation in respect to sex and violence on television, abortion, stem-cell research, and single-sex unions ("gay marriage").[5] Overarching the entire moral values debate was a posture first articulated by the early religious settlers: moral choices are ones of conscience, and governments must not intervene in this private realm. This long historical reach of the ascetic Protestant churches and sects into the twenty-first century, as mediated and rejuvenated by nineteenth-century civic associations, is widely apparent.[6]

Much more successfully than John Kerry, George Bush created an image of his present and past as in conformity with this asceticism-rooted constellation of behavioral standards. Moreover, his capacity to convey direct and uncomplicated proposals to social problems, which contributed to an image of "frankness and candor," far surpassed John Kerry's ability to do so; on the contrary, the senator from Massachusetts was regularly accused of obscurity and inconsistency. The Bush campaign cultivated an image of strength and certainty for its candidate, and John Kerry was portrayed as a "fuzzy," vacillating, and unreliable thinker, prone to embrace contradictory proposals.

Voters repeatedly complained, "one doesn't know where [Kerry] stands" and regularly praised the "trustworthiness and directness" of George W. Bush. The same questions were raised repeatedly: "Where does Kerry stand?" "Where is his moral backbone? His integrity?" "What are his standards and convictions?" "Why are his answers to moral questions complex rather than straightforward?" "Will he allow the government to make fundamentally private decisions?" Surely the reins of power could not be handed over to someone lacking a firm resolve and liable to switch positions frequently—not least because such "flip-flopping," in the end in the American political culture conjured up doubts regarding the candidate's ethics, character, and capacity for decisiveness. The nation must be guided, the Bush campaign asserted, by a resolute leader, acting with consistency on behalf of trusted values. "Good" and "evil" *are* clear-cut and must be proclaimed without uncertainty or ambivalence, Bush insisted. Strength of character demanded doing so.

In a political landscape influenced to this day by the "strong moral character" and "trustworthiness" themes, the unwavering message itself acquired a positive valence. Asceticism's wide resonance, in just these ways, demonstrates the enduring heuristic utility of the generalization model.

The Professional Associations Model: The Relocation and Narrowing of the Sect Legacy

In contrast to the generalization model, the professional associations construct shares a pivotal presupposition with the Weberian construct: American society's metamorphosis has led to a massive expansion of practical rationalism. However, the Weberian model rejects the central presupposition of the professional associations construct: ascetic Protestantism's singular achievement—the sublimation and rationalization of work *across many groups and strata* from a sheer utilitarian activity into a values-based and even sanctified activity—has been eviscerated in the postwar era. Rather, and even though acknowledging labor's longer-term decoupling from value configurations, the professional associations model hypothesizes that Puritanism's legacies permeate deeply into this era. Nonetheless, their *scope* fails to rival the broad expanse achieved by these legacies, as visible in the generalization model. The professional associations construct first articulates their *circumscribed location* in the postwar United States and then examines their continuing influence.

According to this model, a generalization of the ascetic Protestant heritage to the same magnitude as characteristic of the nineteenth century is no longer apparent. Moreover, sect legacies become significantly separated from civic associations—which become more porous and internally less rigorous, this construct maintains. A specific *sector* of American society now becomes the home for these legacies: its upper-middle-class professional associations. Here they are cultivated and sustained, this model contends. As carried by these secular organizations, a values-based orientation to vocations competes directly with practical-rational orientations. How do, according to this construct, postwar professional associations manifest sect legacies?[7]

Acceptable behavior and appropriate moral conduct for members are prescribed. An orientation to high standards must characterize behavior. The admission candidate's suitable conduct is testified to by certificates of educational attainment (rather than a minister's letter of recommendation), which provide the basis for membership. In turn, behavior is monitored formally and informally for its integrity and conformity to the organization's standards. The sect's external form is adopted on this behalf: observational mechanisms and discipline are apparent.

Articulated in "codes of conduct," rules and statutes become enforced by designated committees empowered to punish violators. Penalties can be imposed, including the loss of membership, and severe sanctions may bring careers to a sudden conclusion. Finally, professionals measure their self-worth and dignity against a set of moral codes. Does the member "live up to" the association's standards? Has "professional integrity" been maintained in regard to specific cases and also throughout a career? A sincere "professionalism," and "the professional career" distinctly separated from other realms, here acquires legitimacy and prestige. The values-based foundation of the professional association is maintained in this manner, and values-oriented conduct is incumbent upon members (see Barber 1978–1979; Abbott 1983; Friedson 1984; Abel and Lewis 1989; Sullivan 1995; Brint 1994).

Hence, this model comprehends the professional association as abundantly manifesting sect legacies.[8] A great variety of vocation-based associations have crystallized in the United States, many of which predate the postwar period: for example, the American Medical Association, the American Bar Association, the American Psychological Association, the American Association of Social Workers, and the American Sociological Association. Business corporations large and

small define, and seek to implement, business ethics, codes of conduct, and "mission statements" (see Barber 1978–1979; Abbott 1983;
Friedson 1984; Abel 1985, 1986; Parsons 2007).[9] "Business ethics" and
"legal ethics" classes are offered in business and law schools.

According to this model, the location of ascetic Protestantism's legacies today in professional associations implies significant consequences
for the American civic sphere. A transformation of the sect spirit's
relationship to American society generally has occurred. Its legacies,
this construct hypothesizes, instead of setting standards of good conduct *for a civic sphere* in an expansive way, as did both practical-ethical
individualism and the civic association in the nineteenth century, are
now more narrowly located: members of professional associations are
their social carriers. And because a cultivation of ethical action now
occurs *outside* the civic sphere, its rejuvenation in a manner parallel to
previous centuries—as civic individualism—is precluded. Furthermore,
as a consequence of the internal orientation of professional association
members, these organizations, compared with sects, churches, and
civic associations, evidence a weakened capacity to challenge practical rationalism, Europeanization, and the power of goods. A vacuum
appears in the civic realm. Indeed, this model maps a decoupling of
the sect legacy from the civic arena and hypothesizes the end of ascetic
Protestantism's long-term capacity to nourish civic life. A cultivation
of the spirit of American democracy is absent.

This absence of a *linkage* between professional organizations and the
civic sphere implies an exclusive orientation of members' behavior to
ethical standards and codes of conduct *internal* to these associations.
In addition, this construct hypothesizes that a relationship of antagonism develops between these realms wherever a methodical work ethos
among professionals acquires a halo of "honor," "self-fulfillment," and
"self-realization": itself a legacy of ascetic Protestant values, this legiti-
mating aura bestows further autonomy and prestige upon professional
life.[10] Activities such as civic engagement are not only curtailed owing
to scarce energy and time, according to this model, but also as a result
of their loss, to professionals, of an overtly values-based foundation.[11]

In sum,[12] this construct postulates that the growth in the twentieth
century of practical rationalism, the power of goods, and Europeanization never eradicated ascetic Protestantism's legacies. However, their

manifestation exclusively in the postwar era's professional associations failed to convey practical-ethical action into the civic realm of sufficient intensity to counteract the spread of utilitarian, interest-oriented activity. In stark opposition to the generalization model, the professional associations construct hypothesizes a curtailment of the sect spirit's more far-reaching capacity to call forth a demarcated civic sphere infused by political-ethical action.

The Conflict Model: The Contested Civic Sphere

This construct articulates further hypotheses designed to define the American civic arena's expanse. It contributes the final model to this array. Taken together, they make up a unique spectrum.

Conflict here appears on a regular basis, and competition across groups of approximately equal weight are characteristic. The rejuvenation that originates from crosscutting tensions and rivalries— allegiances of group members are strengthened—sustains a vibrant cultivation of pluralistic groups and a societal openness. Conflict originates in several major ways in the American political culture.

First, conflicts arise from the values of the American worldview. For Weber, inherent to worldviews (*Weltbilder*) is a constellation of values that assumes a great comprehensiveness: they offer answers to ultimate questions. What is the meaning of life? What purpose does our existence serve? How do we best live our lives? Why do suffering, injustice, and misery persist (1968, p. 450; see pp. 439, 450–451, 519)?[13]

The values of the American worldview stand in a relationship of severe antagonism. The pulsating energy of its value configuration emerges in part from a series of "contrasting rules of the game" (Lynd 1967, p. 59). Egalitarianism is praised, yet also are leadership, creativity, individual achievement, and cultivation of the "unique self." Individualism, personal ambition, the pursuit of wealth, and self-reliance are placed upon a pedestal, yet also are civic responsibility, philanthropic giving, participation in one's community, and the cultivation of a service ethos of volunteerism. Widespread hopefulness regarding the future and its "opportunities" prevails, yet also does a strong pragmatism that defends established practices. An expansive risk-taking is revered, yet also is a cautious and utilitarian posture. Honesty, candor, and ethical behavior are esteemed, yet also are shrewdness and a pragmatic approach to problems that awards importance to practical interests; social conformity is ubiquitous and intense, yet also are "rugged individualism," "going your own way," self-reliance, a comparatively broad tolerance for diverse styles of life, and a strong skepticism toward authority. The pursuit of wealth is extolled, yet even the possession of great riches fails to bestow legitimacy upon a self-identification as fundamentally superior to others.

The extent to which these antagonisms become overt varies depending on hosts of political, economic, social, and cultural variations—and their multidimensional interactions. However, inconsistencies seldom remain dormant; they contribute to a feature of American society universally commented on by European observers even prior to Tocqueville and Weber: its restless, pulsating, and dynamic energy.[14] As persons grapple with "dilemmas" and "injustices," and attempt—through reason and cognitive skills generally—to synthesize contradictory components in the American worldview, thrusts are placed into motion that contribute to the formation of diverse interest, political, social, religious, and ethnic groups. In various ways, all of these groups seek to address inconsistencies in this worldview and to offer programs and policies on behalf of amelioration—or "justice." Tensions and conflicts arise perpetually amid this dynamism of competing groups; indeed, as noted, group competition itself reinvigorates group boundaries and leads to a more intense dynamism.

The American political culture's singular constellation—an extreme emphasis on individual rights, self-reliance, and a limited state intertwined with political-ethical action anchored in varieties of civic associations and oriented to civic ideals of community improvement and social trust—energizes citizens and nourishes a vigorous and omnipresent activism and volunteer spirit. The distinctiveness of this political culture, rather than being defined by a predominant orientation on the one hand to the state or on the other hand to practical rationalism's utilitarian calculations, can be discovered in a recurring capacity to identify and act on—through multitudes of civic associations—inconsistencies perceived as severe between an "unjust" empirical reality and civic ideals.

The *discrepancy*, for example, between ideals of universal equality and a common experiencing of inequality and discrimination *itself* repeatedly provided an impulse for reformist causes. The abolitionist, suffrage, civil rights, women's, and gay social movements offer examples.

This central aspect of the American political culture must be directly acknowledged: namely, its broad, associations-based activism and sustained capacity—owing to the perception of *ideals* in a demarcated civic sphere—to rejuvenate practical-ethical action. In this manner, barriers against a comprehensive and enduring withdrawal of citizens from the civic realm are erected. Nonetheless, a potentially dangerous element existed at the core of this political culture: the wide expanse—and, at times, powerful influence and even *obligatory* character—of civic ideals implies the possibility that activity oriented to their fulfillment may intensify and develop into campaigns of moral purification. Indeed, this potential becomes manifest at regular intervals, owing to the persistence of ascetic Protestantism and its secularized legacies, all of which orient activity in a disciplined manner toward these civic ideals.

Herein lie the uniqueness of the American political culture and its central dilemma. Perpetual moral campaigns that point to discrepancies between civic ideals and empirical realities alone rejuvenate the practical-ethical activity at the core of this political culture and in turn restrain the expansion of a divisive practical rationalism deriving from self-interested activity in the political and economic spheres. However, such crusades inject an element of intolerance and may pose a direct threat to personal liberties held dear for more than two hundred years. They may also diminish the vibrant social and political pluralism rooted in American society's multitudes of civic associations.

Appearing with great regularity, moral campaigns in the United States have normally taken relatively innocuous forms devoid of a high potential to disrupt the delicate balance. Campaigns against inequality, discrimination, crime, corruption, alcohol, drugs, tobacco, pornography, prostitution, and big government, for example, can be seen in this light. Occasionally, however, they may become virulent missions "against evil" (McCarthyism, the "evil axis") that acquire the intensity of a crusade.[15]

At times, according to the conflict model, this civic sphere dynamism confronts and restricts the privatization of work, the intensification of the power of goods, bureaucratization, and the circumscription of sect legacies to professional associations. Although never dominant, practical-ethical action continues to be nourished amid regular confrontations and "culture wars," this construct holds. Older ideals—"service to a community"—and a community-building element retain a considerable influence—namely, to constrain practical rationalism significantly.

Hence, in strict opposition to the Weberian construct, the conflict model postulates that the civic sphere continues to exist, albeit to a less substantive extent than hypothesized by the generalization model and although perpetually beset by antagonisms. Powerful civic associations sustain this arena, according to this construct, and the civic realm permeates influential organizations. The spirit of American democracy may be nourished.

Nonetheless, the conflict model hypothesizes that challenges and threats to the civic sphere's existence are unceasing. Its boundaries become less firm. Practical-rational, interest-oriented activity develops more intensively than postulated by the generalization construct. Hence, unconstrained by practical-ethical action to the same extent, utilitarian considerations more frequently orient activity. Furthermore, secularization has banished world-mastery individualism, this model postulates, the halo of sanctity around work, and all God-oriented community building. A depletion of the civic arena's thick quality follows. Accordingly, fewer hindrances obstruct the permeation of daily life by the power of goods. Moreover, the civic realm's independence is contested on a regular basis as bureaucratization proceeds. In these circumstances, a generalization of the ethical action cultivated in professional organizations is precluded; rather, it retains its exclusively internal focus.

The generalization, professional associations, and conflict models expand the Weberian model's analytic framework. All models have formulated arrays of operationalizable hypotheses capable of orienting the empirical investigation of the American political culture even today, the contours and transformations of its civic sphere, and the expanse of its spirit of democracy.

In combination, these constructs define a *spectrum* that conceptualizes the full range of the civic arena's past and present movements. More thick, expansive, and independent manifestations of this realm are apparent at one end of this heuristic tool; more porous, circumscribed, and dependent forms of this sphere anchor the other. Moreover, when taken as a mechanism to orient research, this differentiated conceptual framework can be used to identify directional movements, coalitions across groups, and conflicts across groups. *Arrays* of causally effective groups "carry" movement across this spectrum, Weber insists (see Kalberg 1994, pp. 52–78, 168–176).

His models indicate that an independent civic sphere endures with greater likelihood if rooted in competing groups and regular, pluralistic tensions (Weber 2005, pp. 168–172, 255–271). Sustained, moderate-level conflict facilitates societal openness; ossification occurs with greater probability wherever a single group or organization acquires hegemony, he holds.

In this respect, the bureaucracy's certified, risk-averse, and con-formist functionaries constitute a central problem—yet not one of overwhelming magnitude. A society's stagnation looms more likely whenever *bureaucratization* proceeds to such an extent that few social, economic, political, or legal constraints stand effectively against this development—one that will eventually lead to the substitution of deci-sion making in reference to values by decision making in reference to pragmatic, utilitarian, and instrumental considerations (Weber 2005, pp. 255–271; Kalberg 2011c, pp. 348–356). The civic sphere will then be diminished in scope, as will the American spirit of democracy. Typi-cally, while examining the adverse consequences of bureaucratization, Weber acknowledges a paradox: although they hold bureaucratization in check, dynamic and tension-filled societies today strengthen the power of goods and practical rationalism's unbounded individualism. As discussed, both will also lead to a circumscription of the civic sphere.

Notes

1. Although not exhaustive, these constructs, it is here maintained, constitute the most plausible models to be derived from Weber's conceptual armament.

2. Among the many recent volumes that see an expansion of the civic arena today beyond its traditional manifestations, see Dalton 2008 and Schudson 1998.

3. This model approximates the major presuppositions of the Parsonsian vision of American society. From the point of view of the "pluralistic models" theorizing undertaken here and in Chapter 5, Parsonsian theorizing on American society diverges distinctly: although it also emphasizes that a pendulum movement occurs across a spectrum, its breadth is drastically foreshortened. Hence, compared with Weber, Parsons offers a far more monolithic and harmonious vision of American society and political culture, one rooted in a clear presupposition: levels of integration and of cooperation across various "institutions" are high. Furthermore, whereas Parsons sees the expansion of values ("value-generalization") in the United States as empirically extensive, Weber insists that any such development depends on the empirical presence of multiple carrier groups and facilitating causal constellations. See Parsons 1966, 1971, 2007.

4. Bellah's charting out of an American "civil religion" neglects entirely the asceticism component at its foundation. Indeed, absent this element, a rejuvenation of this civil religion (through holidays, etc.) would occur only in constricted forms, Weber would contend. See Bellah 1970, 1975.

5. According to polls, 63 percent of parents were very concerned regarding the depiction of sex on television, 53 percent regarding the depiction of violence.

6. Hence, an entire set of voter considerations central in European political campaigns was pushed to the margins; namely, competency as measured by professional expertise and command over a body of knowledge. Whereas both Al Gore and John Kerry proved masters of the obscure minutiae of innumerable policy fields, George Bush possessed only a weak command of the major issues—yet this never proved detrimental. A further analysis of cross-cultural variation in respect to the salience and importance of specialized knowledge in electoral campaigns would need to emphasize not only the ascetic Protestant heritage, but also an array of additional factors, such as the influence of the American "achievement society," characterized by comparatively high levels of long-range occupational mobility and open labor markets, as well as widespread populism and social egalitarianism. All contribute significantly to the populism-grounded American mistrust of professional politicians, policy experts, government bureaucrats, and intellectuals.

7. Of course, such professional associations are also found in other countries. They have originated, however, either from the laws of a state or the leadership initiative of elite groups rather than from a broad-based sect heritage. See Rueschemeyer 1973; Abel 1985, 1986; Abel and Lewis 1989.

8. If Weber had lived to observe the full development and scope of the professional association, he would have viewed it also from another vantage point—namely, as offering further support for his fundamental position: any

characterization of American society as a sandpile of unconnected individuals is flawed (see Kalberg 2011b).

9. Merton's classic statement vividly renders the sect legacy in the case of the professionalism of "the man of science": "The ethos of science is that affectively toned complex of values and norms which is held to be binding on the man of science. The norms are expressed in the form of prescriptions, proscriptions, preferences and permissions. They are legitimatized in terms of institutional values. These imperatives, transmitted by precept and example and reinforced by sanctions, are in varying degrees internalized by the scientist, thus fashioning his scientific conscience. . . . Although the ethos of science has not been codified, it can be inferred from the moral consensus of scientists as expressed in use and wont, in countless writings on the scientific spirit, and in moral indignation directed toward contraventions of this ethos" (1973, pp. 268–269).

10. Sullivan correctly derives the lineage of professionalism today from Weber's notion of (a Puritan) vocation. However, his interesting argument—a "civic professionalism" is undergoing aggrandizement and offers the promise to rejuvenate the civic sphere—diverges from the position just demarcated: a substantial *linkage* between professional organizations and the civic sphere must be apparent. See Sullivan 1995, pp. 191–237. Steven Brint's notion of "social trustee professionalism" parallel's Sullivan's position (see Brint 1994), Weber's position is clear: adequate social carriers (see Chapter 5) for such an *expansion* of the professional ethos into the civic sphere are absent.

11. With the exception of South Korea, Americans now work more hours per year than the people of any other nation. Although acknowledging the important causal weight of external constraint and domination, Weber's sociology insists that a consideration of cultural contexts must also be included in any causal explanation. See Kalberg 1994, 2012.

12. An empirical substantiation of this model would require comparative investigation. It would postulate that professional associations in other nations assume a less activist posture in respect to both the monitoring of members and effective punishment measures than their American counterparts. Moreover, the power to impose penalties for "unprofessional conduct" usually lies in other nations with legal authorities outside the association (see Rueschemeyer 1973; Abel and Lewis 1989; Savelsberg 1994, 1999; Savelsberg and King 2005).

13. A worldview's value constellation may be, according to Weber, grounded in either the supernatural or "worldly" realms. Intellectual, social, and political movements, as well as religions, may offer broad-ranging sets of values and an "ordered meaningfulness." Once established, worldviews erect a *disjunction* between the empirical "worldly realm," on the one hand, and an ethical order of coherent values and pronounced ideals, on the other hand.

Hence, the values of the worldview stand in strict opposition to all (a) diffuse and random action, (b) means-end rational, strategic action, and (c) tradition-oriented action. For a more comprehensive definition of worldviews, following Weber, see Kalberg 2012, pp. 73–92.

14. As Tocqueville notes, "The whole life of an American is passed like a game of chance, a revolutionary crisis, or a battle" (1945, vol. 1, p. 443).

15. At times these crusades may even assume the appropriateness of indigenous ideals and values—for they are perceived by Americans as universal—for peoples of other cultures (Hofstadter 1967). (On the rootedness of prominent missionary idealism elements in American foreign policy in the American political culture, see Kalberg 1991, 2003.) *Nonetheless*, and although maintenance of the delicate balance between political-ethical reinvigoration and personal liberties continuously presents severe challenges to the American political culture, and the vast pluralism of its civic associations implies enduring conflict, any lessening of the tension underlying this balance contains profoundly disruptive consequences: a foundational *source* of the characteristic American vigor, dynamism, and openness would then come under attack. Scientific, cultural, political, and economic innovation are facilitated by this delicate balance, vast pluralism, and enduring, yet moderate, conflict. This balance also facilitates the assimilation of this nation's diverse and numerous minorities, a periodic and measured critique of the status quo, and gradualist capacities that sustain social reform agendas and inhibit revolutionary movements.

CHAPTER SEVEN

Conclusion

Max Weber's Analysis of the
Spirit of American Democracy,
Past, Present, and Future

> One must ... focus upon what is of central importance in a society, despite
> all analogies, and use the similarities of two societies to highlight the specific
> individuality of each. This specificity is always discernible.
>
> —*Weber 1976, p. 341*

VOICES THAT PROCLAIM an "American crisis" have
reverberated loudly over the last fifteen years. At times,
dire warnings have monopolized the media. An excessive
individualism and lower rates of participation in civic groups are
lamented. More and more Americans are "bowling alone," Robert
Putnam argues (2000).

Moreover, the post-2008 era of massive wealth inequality and
domination by powerful elites, very recent critics insist, has led to a
withering of the American Dream. In this "New Gilded Age," upward
mobility will soon assume the form of a utopian ideal, they hold (see
Stiglitz 2012; Reich 2011, 2012), and the civic sphere's capacity to
call forth public service values and a "shared community" will vanish.

A fading of all notions of self-reliance will follow, as well as a severe privatization of life.

This study has sought to introduce into this discussion a long-range perspective—a historical dimension—too often downplayed by this "crisis commentary." Concepts well-equipped to link the distant past to the present have been used throughout: the American *political culture* and *spirit of democracy.* These concepts expand our understanding of the major contours of the American political landscape today, it has been argued, beyond that offered by the crisis commentary.

However, the focus here on this political culture has not only served to convey the ways in which the American past tightly links to the American present; it has also grounded a further central goal of this study: to inject, on behalf also of a better comprehension of the present, a *mode of analysis* anchored in clear concepts and procedures. The present-day crisis discussion lacks such a systematic approach. By reference to both the massive impact of the past on the present *and* a rigorous mode of analysis, this study has provided a more multidimensional and systematic discussion of the present-day American political landscape than that offered by the crisis commentary.

Our goal to inject a historical dimension presented a task of daunting complexity. Indispensable guidance was provided by Max Weber's mode of analysis and his unequivocal stance: political cultures are rooted deeply in a nation's past and constitute long-range causal forces. They demonstrate remarkable resilience and staying power on the basis of their largely indigenous value constellations; the past continuously and powerfully imprints the present, he maintains. Indeed, using unique concepts and procedures, Weber formulated a clear definition of the early American spirit of democracy and offered explanations for its sources, value content, development, and eventual circumscription. He also provided research tools that charted its long historical reach.

His mode of analysis revealed how the political culture dominant in the Colonial era and the early United States formed the foundation for this spirit of democracy. The constellation of *beliefs and values* that undergirded this epoch's accustomed conduct of politics came to the forefront throughout his analysis. A *particular* frame of mind, or ethos, influenced broadly the political views of Americans, he maintains. Here we discovered a singular tenor and extent of civic participation, as well as the habitus of Americans in respect to authority, equality, the competition of pluralistic groups, and self-governance in general. Not least, Weber's mode of analysis articulated, and defined clearly, the unique symbiotic dualisms indigenous to this political culture. All previous chapters have sought to clarify how, according to Weber, the American political culture crystallized and then helped to sustain, through its spirit of democracy, self-governance mechanisms over the long term.

A number of now-familiar themes and queries assumed a central position. How did the political values and beliefs of the seventeenth and eighteenth centuries originate? What was their precise content? To what degree was the birth and 220-year history of American democracy influenced by a supportive spirit of democracy? Have its major elements now, at the beginning of the twenty-first century, undergone a transformation, as the crisis commentary asserts? If so, has a new configuration replaced the long-enduring spirit of democracy and begun to influence the functioning of democracy in the United States in a disruptive and harmful manner? Chapters 5 and 6 outlined various ways in which this spirit may influence the contours of American democracy *today*. They also examined a diverse array of challenges and threats to this spirit.

Analyses undertaken by contributors to the recent crisis literature offer a different focus. Their emphasis on problems confronting present-day America has largely neglected the important part played by this nation's political culture. This volume has argued that, although important, the familiar themes referred to by these authors (see pp. 3–4)—the economic and political interests of powerful actors in groups, the post-2008 radical inequality and the concentration of wealth in the hands of a tiny few, and a colonization of the civic sphere by elites, for example—omit too much. In particular, two concerns of crucial centrality here are downplayed by the crisis commentators: (a) the unique contours of a political culture that assisted the growth of an American spirit of democracy *over several epochs*, and (b) the significant impact of this spirit on modes of self-governance in the United States *throughout its history*.

This chapter first reviews the major themes and arguments presented in Chapters 1 through 6. We then turn to the question of whether *lessons* can be drawn from Weber's analysis regarding (a) the origins, development, and features of the American political culture; (b) its impact, through its spirit of democracy, on the birth and growth of American democracy; and (c) its influence today. Has the focus here upon a single political culture assisted comprehension of the ways in which democracy-supportive political cultures crystallize *generally?* Has it provided insight into the ways in which stable democracies originate and develop? Once authoritarian rulership has fragmented, do participation-oriented, civic-based, and citizen-driven political cultures arise organically? Weber's analysis of the American political culture must be first reexamined.

Reviewing the Argument

A Colonial Era Symbiotic Dualism

Members of ascetic Protestant sects and churches were deeply and comprehensively engaged in "the religious life." Asceticism's demands loosened even bonds to the family, Weber contends. The Puritan faithful toiled together on behalf of a joint purpose: to erect a Kingdom of God on earth that would, owing to its abundance and justice, praise unequivocally His majesty and righteousness. *His community* must be constructed.

As argued in Chapters 1, 2, and 3, Weber insists that the *origins* of an American civic sphere and a practical-ethical individualism deeply permeated by values[1] can be discovered in the typical activities undertaken by the devout in these sects and churches. The perpetual orientation of believers to the question of their personal salvation was central, he contends.[2]

A Colonial era *symbiotic dualism* also proved crucial. In this epoch, ascetic Protestantism's intensive community-building efforts and world-mastery individualism reciprocally interacted. Significant consequences followed from this mutual affirmation: the Puritan faithful acquired the self-confidence that bolstered their capacity to confront in His name obstacles and difficulties, ethical action circumscribed practical-rational—or utilitarian—action in a sustained manner, and a frame of mind was formed that consistently upheld activity, even if unpopular, oriented to commandments and principles.

Weber firmly rejects all arguments that explain the origin and intensity of this symbiotic dualism as an evolutionary residual of societal differentiation, value generalization, "progress," democracy's egalitarianism, or the growth of capitalism and the expansive economic interests of its ruling class. The sources of this dualism's axes must be understood, he argues, as located in confrontations by devout believers with the urgent *salvation question* posed by ascetic Protestantism's doctrine of Predestination and view of God (see Chapter 2). Furthermore, this early symbiotic dualism nourished *both* world-mastery individualism and community building to such a profound extent that legacies were laid down, Weber holds—indeed ones that imprinted the nineteenth century deeply. Indebted to Puritanism, a new linkage became clear in this era between a secularized ideal community—a civic sphere—and world-mastery individualism's most forceful manifestation in this century. This *new* symbiotic dualism called forth, Weber is convinced, a *values-based*, civic-oriented individualism empowered to confront— and even restrict—practical rationalism's interest-oriented pursuits and pragmatic calculations.

The Nineteenth Century: A Civic-Oriented Individualism and a New Symbiotic Dualism

Throughout the nineteenth century, American individualism continued to be directed to a significant degree toward civic activity, Weber maintains. Multitudes of cohesive associations permeated this society. Far from a "sandpile of unconnected atoms," Americans lived deeply within—although not fully subordinated to—civic groups. They oriented action in an influential manner. These groups did so in some cases in an overtly ethical way, he contends (see Chapter 4).

This *new* symbiotic dualism was constituted from a thick civic sphere on the one hand and a practical-ethical—or civic-oriented— individualism on the other hand. It gave rise to a spirit of democracy permeated by, Weber insists (see Chapters 4 and 5), *ideals* of goodwill, civic participation, social trust, egalitarianism, civic responsibility, and a consistent support for standards and principles.[3] Moreover, the capacity of this civic arena perpetually to rejuvenate practical-ethical individualism—and its capacity in turn to nourish and sustain civic groups and the civic sphere—proved unique, Weber teaches.[4] The developmental pathways and dynamics of American democracy were significantly grounded in this new dualism, he argues. Its mutually affirming components compose important beliefs and values underpinning the daily conduct of politics.[5]

To a significant extent, American *politics* acquired an ethical dimension in this manner in the nineteenth century. *Ethical* ideals expanded beyond their accustomed location in the nuclear and extended family and into a civic sphere. To the same degree, they challenged the practical rationalism widespread in the economy and political arenas (see Weber 1946c, pp. 331–340; 1968, pp. 346, 585, 1186). The consequence to Weber was evident: both realms became again penetrated by values and transformed. Conversely, the modernizing German political culture located practical-ethical action less expansively. On the one hand, it became manifest divisively in working-class movements of the late nineteenth century and political parties articulating either Left or Right worldviews, and on the other hand, in the universal laws[6] of a developing social welfare state (see Chapter 4, pp. 63–65).[7]

In the nineteenth century, movement across an American spectrum, anchored at its boundaries by a practical-ethical individualism and a viable civic sphere, sustained a spirit of democracy that supported self-governance, Weber contends. It opposed clearly the iron cage dichotomy: here a public sphere lacking both a viable civic sphere and this civic-oriented individualism, and pervaded by technical, administrative, and market constraints as well as hierarchical social conventions, raw power, and calculations of interests, stood opposite an apolitical, deeply private refuge where intimate relations of warmth and compassion were cultivated (see Chapter 5).[8] The American configuration also starkly diverged from those political cultures in which civil service functionaries, the state's laws, and closed political parties encompassed and monopolized the public sphere.[9]

As noted (see Chapters 2–4), the interest-oriented, utilitarian individual remains incapable, according to Weber, of giving birth to the disciplined, values-based action he sees as indispensable to the formation and nourishment of a civic sphere. Indeed, he argues that this arena cannot *endure* wherever a practical-ethical individualism is absent and a symbiotic relationship between the civic realm and this civic-oriented individualism is lacking. Thus, devoid of consistent internal guidance by values, practical-rational individualism must be rationalized into this practical-ethical individualism if a civic sphere is to congeal and last.

To Weber, in other words, endowed with great continuity and rigor from its values component and asceticism heritage, as well as a powerful community-building capacity, practical-ethical individualism exclusively possesses the capacity to defend and uphold—especially against the flux and flow of popular opinion—civic ideals and a civic sphere of substance. As this individualism does so, it rejuvenates both these ideals and this sphere.[10] *Only* asceticism and asceticism-rooted legacies proved strong enough to anchor a type of individualism capable of erecting, cultivating, and reinvigorating a civic sphere over longer periods, Weber contends.[11]

Moreover, he further insists that a singular capacity of these values, in comparison with practical-rational, interest-oriented action, must be explicitly recognized: if supported by cohesive carrier groups such as sects, churches, and civic associations, civic-oriented values provide *continuity* across generations and even centuries.[12] By pulling individuals away from sheer utilitarian and pragmatic postures in an enduring manner, they serve as sustaining cornerstones to American democracy. *This* values-based and civic-oriented individualism, Weber maintains, came to predominantly characterize the American political culture and spirit of democracy.[13] *Values* stand at the foundation of its mode of self-governance, he teaches, rather than the random sway of interests and power.[14]

Nonetheless, Weber attends repeatedly to the empirical fragility of the nineteenth-century symbiotic dualism and the delicate balancing it required (see Chapters 3–4). Perpetual social change in the twentieth century also endangered the practical-ethical individualism–civic sphere symbiosis and foretold polarization and fragmentation. As its reciprocity weakened and intensity dissolved, its two axes increasingly assumed independent routes. As linkages became eviscerated, both became exposed and vulnerable (see Chapters 5–6). Thus, *external* elements increasingly determined the expansion and contraction of these axes: domination constellations, interest-based alignments, and the steady flow of power. Wherever the civic sphere becomes porous and loses its ethical dimension, a certain development likely follows, Weber argues: a greater probability arises for practical-ethical action to become routinized back to practical-rational orientations.

Lessons from the Unusual American Case?

This review of Weber's analysis of the origins, value content, trajectories, and impact of the American political culture's spirit of democracy has indicated how a complex mixture of values, beliefs, and symbiotic dualisms, according to him, undergird and sustain American democracy. This *political culture* has exercised a long-term and positive impact on democracy in the United States and influenced its unusual features, he contends.[15] To a significant extent, its origin and longevity must be comprehended as anchored in the religious values and salvation goals of Puritanism, Weber holds, rather than in purely mundane factors such as the Constitution's checks, balances, and formal procedures (such as elections), the rational choices of atomistic individuals, and the political and economic interests of powerful groups.

The influence of ascetic Protestantism on the origins of American democracy appears singular, and the symbiotic dualisms of the Colonial era and nineteenth century appear unique. The same must be concluded regarding their impact. And the particular *interaction* of this spirit in the twentieth century with mass urbanization, modern capitalism, industrialization, and the aggrandizement of wealth in the hands of a small elite, as explored in Chapters 4 through 6, also constitutes a distinctly American experience. Can this investigation of this political culture's major sources, features, trajectory, and particular impact on American democracy's formation and development formulate lessons concerning the birth and endurance of new democracies generally? Are American history and American dualisms so unusual that their transposition to nations moving today from authoritarianism to democracy is precluded? Weber's position on this score is clear: extreme caution must be exercised.

His methodology rejects such "generalization" from a single case. *Every* route to modern democracy is distinct, he maintains.[16] Thus, his case orientation would energetically oppose two positions that might now appear plausible: (a) democracies arise and develop *only* on the foundation of a Puritanism-based political culture and (b) nations anchored in different political cultures will follow trajectories toward authoritarian rulership. For example, in both England and France, democracies originated from social configurations quite unlike those in America. Moreover, both of these nations pursued distinct pathways, according to Weber. Until the twentieth century, a highly centralized administrative state and Catholicism characterized France, and in England the (anti-Puritan) Anglican Church and a decentralized rulership by a rural aristocratic class—the gentry—prevailed for centuries (see Weber 1968, pp. 1059–1064; Bendix 1978, pp. 292–320).[17]

Weber's mode of analysis opposes all schools that pronounce democracy's "overarching pathway" or "uniform roadmap." His sociology rejects all "single model" methodologies and pursues a different course: it constructs concepts and procedures *for the rigorous study of single cases* and their impact over longer periods of time. The methodology used above in order to explain the origins, value content, and development of a particular spirit of democracy in a single nation, and its long-term influence, constitutes an *application* of his mode of analysis. It has sought to convey the manner in which *Weber would have investigated*, had he undertaken to do so in a rigorous manner, the sources, values, development, and impact of the American political culture.

Commentaries on Weber's works have frequently obscured the orientation of his research to discrete problems and the causal analysis of specific cases and developments.[18] He proposes that an explanation of the uniqueness and rise of the "historical individual" should serve as sociology's primary aim: "We wish to understand the reality that surrounds our lives, in which we are placed, *in its characteristic uniqueness*" (1949, p. 72, translation altered, original emphasis, see also p. 69; 1968, p. 10; 2011c, pp. 76–77).

Hence, Weber stands against the numerous positivist schools of thought in his day that sought, following the experimental methodology of the natural sciences, to discover a set of general societal laws and to explain specific developments by deduction from them. He rejected forcefully the position that the social sciences should aim "to construct a closed system of concepts which can encompass and classify reality in some definitive manner and from which it can be deduced again" (1949, p. 84).[19] Furthermore, he expressed directly his antagonism to the view that laws themselves provide causal explanations. Because concrete realities, cases, developments, and subjective meaning cannot be deduced from them, laws remain incapable of providing the knowledge for such explanations, he maintains (1949, pp. 75–76; see Kalberg 1994, pp. 81–84).

Not surprisingly, he fails to offer the prescriptive guidance of crucial importance to many social scientists and political actors today. His sociology neither seeks nor provides laws and axioms that "instruct" persons in respect to "desired" political activity of a certain stripe.[20] If his methodology is to be followed, even the linkages he charts in Chapters 3, 4, and 5 of this text—a sect heritage in Colonial America facilitated the birth of civic associations in the nineteenth century, which then formed a solid foundation for the pluralistic competition of groups supportive of self-governance, for example—cannot be comprehended as "general prerequisites" to be "put into place" as building blocks for stable democracies. Rather, self-governance arose in some nations, Weber holds, where sects and civic associations were absent. And the conclusion he reached in his analysis of democracy's endurance in the United States—a symbiotic dualism between practical-ethical individualism and the civic sphere contributed to the longevity of the American mode of self-governance—must not be formulated either as a "prerequisite" or as a nation-transcending axiom, he admonishes.

Weber's concepts and procedures emphasize the multiple causes behind all historical developments and the indispensability of cohesive and powerful groups as social carriers if patterned action is to become influential. They also lay stress on the ways in which the embeddedness of groups severely inhibits the effectiveness of other groups oriented toward social change (see Kalberg 1994, pp. 98–102, 168–176, 189–192). And the "thickness" of the embeddedness varies. These foundational features of Weber's sociology hinder the easy formation of clear laws and their "general application" across cases.

His attention to the multiple ways in which subjective meaning is formed by persons assembled in innumerable—and often antagonistic—groups also persuaded him to reject the notion that the social sciences appropriately strive to form laws. His view of "societies" did so as well—namely, as constituted from arrays of dynamically interacting groups rather than as organically holistic. Weber's choice of the ideal type as his major heuristic tool confirms this position foundational to his sociology: instead of "society" and its lawfulness, these constructs are oriented toward—and "document"—bounded groups and regularities of patterned action within them. As *models*, they point to probable (and improbable) cross-group, empirical-causal relationships rather than to "society" and its "general laws." In addition, owing to the capacity of these constructs to chart the merging of some groups and the decoupling of others, ideal types regularly capture fluctuating, open-ended tensions and shifting alliances. This aspect of Weber's mode of analysis also opposes the formation of laws.

The Weberian Mode of Analysis: Studying Political Cultures

This volume has argued throughout that Weber's concepts and procedures are of great utility to social scientists investigating the American political culture today. Although, as noted, his conclusions in respect to *this* case cannot be generalized or transferred, his mode of analysis can be readily used—and in a parallel manner—in order to define the values and beliefs at the foundation of other political cultures, as well as to explain their sources, development, and impact. In other words, his concepts and procedures can clearly identify beliefs and values and then explain how some support self-governance and others restrict open participation and democracy in general. Weber's orientation to the empirical investigation of cases and their causes remains, as does his formation of useful concepts.

Hence, he abjures modes of analysis familiar to us today. He opposes, as discussed previously, all broad evolutionary axioms: differentiation, adaptive upgrading, value generalization, and modernization, for example. They level out and downplay, he insists, the complexity of the multiple interwoven processes surrounding each case and each development. Weber's methodology must also be distinguished sharply, as noted, from all schools that seek to understand the origin, stability, and longevity of democracies by reference exclusively to the rational choices of individuals, the checks and balances of a constitution, and the power of certain groups and the state.

Furthermore, as also discussed, checks and balances, citizen demonstrations, formal procedures, and the exhortations by "senior statesmen" and persons "of integrity" and "goodwill" do not give birth to, he contends, nor cultivate systematically and over longer time frames, the beliefs and values supportive of a democracy-oriented political culture. Finally, unlike many sociologists today, Weber maintains that political cultures never result from political or economic forces alone. Even putatively highly conducive external conditions, such as significant social equality, advanced industrialism, and high levels of societal wealth, of themselves fail to *call forth* beliefs and values that sustain self-governance. Research oriented in these directions will yield only surface-level explanations, he argues. The establishment of democracy-supportive political cultures has been complex and rare, Weber insists. Moreover, he emphasizes also that even highly amenable values and beliefs may be circumscribed effectively amid power constellations. This may occur over the short term, though also over the long term.

More than one hundred nations around the globe have modeled their constitutions on the American document. However, in the vast majority of these countries, efforts to establish political cultures that support democracy's functioning have only rarely succeeded. After a decade or two, mechanisms formed at the outset to distribute power through checks and balances have frequently dissolved. Social movements initially inspired by noble ideals have regularly become transformed into organizations oriented to the defense of narrow economic and political interests.

Beginning in February 2011, news of the Arab Spring overwhelmed the media worldwide. Completely unanticipated, a faith in democracy and a spirit in search of egalitarianism proved strong. Hope and idealism ran high, and the wide participation of citizens in their own forms of government appeared immanent. All queried whether the nations of northern Africa and the Middle East possessed political cultures capable of *sustaining* the rule of democracy. If so, would they become influential?

Worrisome events have become all too frequent and given birth to many concerns. It has become evident that the overthrow of autocrats constitutes only the first step, and the formation of self-governance procedures seldom follows a smooth pathway. The Arab Spring's pervasive optimism—"the people will establish a democracy once external coercion and intimidation have ceased"—seems to have almost vanished. Syria's civil war is intense, and Egypt and Libya appear headed down this pathway.

Well-known to students of political cultures, the turning points to be surmounted are many. Old and closed political elites may be replaced by new elites—nearly equally closed. These groups may impose regimes almost as corrupt as the earlier authoritarian rulership, and initial steps toward self-governance may be restricted and reversed by the state's coercive powers. In some regions, religious sectarianism, ethnic strife, and clan rivalries may boil to the surface immediately after the demise of the autocrat's iron rule. In this context, even if somehow formed, a democracy-facilitating political culture will have little effect.

Twenty years ago democracy appeared on the immediate horizon across Eastern Europe. However, political cultures conducive to open, pluralistic institutions and a functioning civic sphere have congealed in only a few of these nations (see Kotkin 2010). Must the individual liberties indigenous to a vibrant civic arena be viewed as only the dreams of intellectuals and dissidents?

As emphasized, Weber argues that an investigation of the rational choices of individuals, the role of the state, the checks and balances required by a constitution, and the interests of elites all fail to address this query adequately—and for a simple reason: it pertains *also* to the composition of a nation's political culture. It relates in particular to its capacity to set into motion a general spirit of democracy, he maintains. *This* political culture *facilitates* the birth of a civic realm, the prolongation of its openness and accessibility, the regular participation of citizens, and representative democracy in general, Weber holds. Yet it may be delicate and short-lived.

The specific yield from this Weberian investigation of *American* democracy's origin and longevity can now be defined succinctly: a particular political culture anchored in a *spirit of democracy enhanced* the possibility that democratic self-governance would congeal and endure. Conversely, this case study rooted in Weber's mode of analysis concludes that greater obstacles will be confronted whenever attempts to establish democracies lack a supportive political culture.

His concepts and procedures have demonstrated that reciprocally sustaining dualisms indigenous to early American beliefs and values "pulled" activities in the Colonies and in the nineteenth century, with some regularity, beyond the random flow of power and utilitarian interests. Indeed, the symbiotic dualisms effective in these epochs focused the energies of Americans to a significant degree on common—even civic—concerns. A fertile field for the growth of heterogeneous civic associations appeared and expanded in the nineteenth century—not least owing to the influence of this era's secular symbiotic dualism. However, significant obstacles crystallized throughout the twentieth century. When applied systematically, Weber's mode of analysis offers insights and explanations that assist comprehension of the origins, value content, development, and impact of the American spirit of democracy.

Although now familiar, four main elements of his approach to the study of political cultures should be stressed. First, it emphasizes that social action may become deeply embedded in values that may significantly influence this action, and that—if to become influential—values must acquire strong social carriers. Second, Weber teaches that, if strong social carriers congeal and remain powerful, values and beliefs possessing roots in past centuries may become viable in the present, indeed even regularly and significantly. Third, a symbiotic dualism between a civic arena and practical-ethical individualism becomes manifest, he holds, only as a consequence of an unusual juxtaposition of multiple factors—yet just this interweaving may become causally significant for the birth and expansion of a political culture that facilitates the formation of a working democracy. Finally, although acknowledging the long-range staying power (should adequate social carriers crystallize) of a political culture's beliefs and values, *and* their capacity to influence the birth and development of democracies, Weber's mode of analysis also calls attention to their vulnerability and fragility.

Notes

1. A brief glance at Tocqueville's understanding of individualism, which varies dramatically from that of Weber, will highlight the uniqueness of Weber's argument. Tocqueville's examination of religion remains almost entirely limited to general discussions regarding the manner in which belief provides standards of behavior and virtue particularly indispensable, if a tyranny of the majority is to be avoided, in periods of increasing egalitarianism (see Tocqueville 1945, vol. 2, pp. 22–29).

For Tocqueville, individualism arises with the decline of feudalism and the subsequent appearance of egalitarianism: "individualism is of democratic origin, and it threatens to spread in the same ratio as the equality of conditions" (vol. 2, p. 104). According to this purely structural argument, equality itself loosens the fixed positions and duties inherent to feudalism's organic stratification and allows persons to view themselves as separate from both the past and all firm societal anchoring: the "bond of human affection is extended, but it is relaxed" (vol. 2, p. 104). Without firm social hierarchies, persons are no longer "links in a chain"; rather, they become disconnected from one another and even strangers: "as social conditions become more equal, the number of persons increases ... [who] owe nothing to any man; they acquire the habit of always considering themselves as standing alone, and they are apt to imagine that their whole destiny is in their own hands" (vol. 2, p. 105; see also pp. 104–107). Unlike organically stratified societies, where persons are strongly connected with one another as a consequence of fixed obligations, duties, and responsibilities, equality implies an isolation of persons one from another, he holds, if only because the clear "sense of place" indigenous to the feudal society is lacking. Fundamentally, Tocqueville defines individualism as involving an isolation of "[the person]—an 'atomism'—[and] concentration of attention upon oneself: ... democracy ... throws him back forever upon himself alone, and threatens in the end to confine him entirely within the solitude of his own heart" (vol. 2, p. 106). Further, "The principle of equality, which makes men independent of each other, gives them a habit and a taste for following in their private actions no other guide than their own will" (p. 304; see also p. 343).

This individualism, far from oriented to world mastery or rooted in the ascetic's rigid adherence to abstract principles and rules, is "enfeebled" and devoid of a clear line of internal direction, for "equality sets men apart and weakens them" (vol. 2, p. 344). Not surprisingly, in his discussions of the various safeguards against a tyranny of the majority, Tocqueville fails to mention individualism. The individualism Weber sees on American soil, anchored in the world-mastery orientations of ascetic Protestant *belief* rather than a social leveling process, diverges dramatically from that of Tocqueville. Further on Tocqueville's harsh descriptions of individualism, see Kalberg 1997, p. 219, n. 9.

2. Tocqueville attends to civic associations rather than a civic sphere, and sees their origin in the "commercial passions" that became manifest with greater egalitarianism, and a pursuit of common economic interests (see Chapter 3, note 15). Departing from this disagreement, a fundamental opposition between these two great theorists can be charted. See, for example, Chapter 1, note 5; Kalberg 1997.

3. That this orientation—to standards and principles—in American political life (as well as in American life in general) must be seen as a direct legacy of Puritanism has been discussed on several occasions above. See in particular Chapters 1, 2, and 6.

4. It is this distinction between a practical-rational individualism and a practical-ethical individualism that foreign observers since Crèvecoeur (1735–1813; see 1981) have seldom understood. Comprehension is rendered more difficult by the wide value pluralism in the United States and the common practice of seeking, in order to resolve disputes, a compromise position. As a consequence of this pragmatic negotiation posture, the belief often prevails among foreign commentators that values are disingenuously held, easily cast aside, and serve only external display purposes. European commentators on the Right are convinced that "no country is *that* advanced" (that is, to elevate the importance of values to such a degree that they very often guide civic-sphere action), and commentators on the Left insist that the high-intensity and advanced development of American capitalism precludes a viable civic sphere.

5. Tocqueville's focus on civic associations can now be seen as inadequate to his overarching goal: to explain the stability of American democracy. His argument—these associations will limit the dangerous passions and restless desires that (putatively) arise with egalitarianism (see 1945, vol. I, pp. 48–55 et passim) and thereby fulfill a basic precondition for the creation of a stable democracy—neglects the symbiotic dualisms at the core of this political culture. Moreover, the power of groups over the individual reaches for Tocqueville—and appropriately so, he contends—a significantly greater intensity than for Weber. Owing to his orientation to subjective meaning, Weber discovers that a reflective person with pluralistic action options *may* appear *even* in extremely cohesive groups (the sect or the bureaucracy, for example). His methodology allows him to see that the power of the sect to influence behavior profoundly results from the *tension* that arises in believers as a consequence of its capacity *to combine* an asceticism-based, "hold your own" individualism with extreme social conformity pressures. See Chapter 2, pp. 39–42. Again, to Weber "there is no stronger means of breeding [ethical]

traits" (2011d, pp. 224–225; 2011a, pp. 230–232). Fundamental differences in their sociological methodologies separate these theorists and lead to clear differences in their analyses of the American political culture (see Kalberg 1997).

6. This statement should not be misunderstood. German society possessed multitudes of groups. However, they were primarily hobby and recreational-leisure groups; that is, they must be understood as privatized rather than as *civic* groups in the sense used here.

7. Not surprisingly, most sociologists in Germany remained blind to both pillars of the American configuration—a civic sphere and practical-ethical action—and, hence, perceived American society as inadequately grounding an expansive, community-building solidarity. Their error (with the exception of Weber)—atomization universally accompanied capitalism and urbanization—must be seen as involving a false transposition onto the United States. This *misperception*, because it implied that all societies undergoing this great transformation to urbanism, modern capitalism, and industrialism are fundamentally similar to German society, occluded cognizance of *each* nation's "exceptionalism." More specifically, German sociologists (as did Crèvecoeur and Tocqueville in France) failed to acknowledge the broad impact of the sect tradition and, in particular, its strong capacity to call forth group formation (see Chapters 1–3; Weber 2011a, pp. 231–232; 2011d, pp. 224–226).

8. Critical theory's attribution of this dichotomy generally to modern capitalism in all industrializing nations constitutes a fundamental misreading of the unusual features of *American* capitalism. See Horkheimer 1972, pp. 188–243; Arato and Gebhardt 1982, pp. 26–48; Marcuse 1964. Parsonsian modernization theory errs in this respect also egregiously—although in the opposite direction.

9. As in Weber's Germany. See 1946b, pp. 103, 111–114; 1968, pp. 1381–1469; 1994.

10. The agenda of some theorists today (see Introduction, note 3)—to weaken and restrict the utilitarian individual and to strengthen and expand the civic sphere—faces, in light of Weber's analysis, poor prospects. Moreover, because they downplay the subjective meaningfulness of action, these commentators remain ill-equipped (a) to evaluate the extent to which activity *varies* in intensity and (b) to acknowledge the ways in which the formation of a viable civic sphere *requires* practical-ethical individualism. Hence, they neglect the *symbiotic* dualisms stressed by Weber as at the core of the American political culture and its spirit of democracy.

11. That many observers today generally fail to take cognizance of a principled, deeply rooted, and values-based individualism in the American political culture is more surprising than is the parallel blindness of their intellectual father: Tocqueville wrote within a European social context saturated

by a general skepticism regarding (a) individualism and (b) the survival of values in the new era of democracy. See Chapter 4, pp. 63–65.

12.   The discussion of Bellah et al. in *Habits of the Heart* (1985) of *four* cultural traditions prominent in American culture—the Biblical, the Republican, the Utilitarian Individualist, and the Expressive Individualist—neglects the many ways in which ascetic Protestantism underlies and connects *all* of these traditions (including the latter—a reaction against Puritanism). Each is treated as if of independent origin. Utilitarian Individualism, for example, is derived (following Tocqueville) from pragmatic and immediate currents and interests rather than from Puritanism's sanctification of work, goal-oriented activity (as long as it is ultimately guided by values), and the search for profit and wealth. (Bellah, in neglecting the wide-ranging and penetrating influences of ascetic Protestantism *and* its unique capacity to inject a qualitatively different—and extremely significant—*intensity* to work and activity, follows directly in Tocqueville's footsteps; see Bellah et al. 1985, pp. 27–35.) Tocqueville repeatedly explains aspects of American society by reference to its "equality of conditions" rather than to the legacies of ascetic Protestantism. Although noting that "innumerable" sects exist on American soil, he maintains that "all Christian morality is everywhere the same" (1945, vol. 1, p. 314; see vol. 2, pp. 22–23, 28). See Kalberg 1997, p. 221, notes 26 and 27.

13.   American civic individualism can now be demarcated clearly vis-à-vis Nietzschean individualism (the individual as the exceptional hero fully separate from "the masses") and the individualism of early-nineteenth-century German Romanticism (the Goethean individual as unique and as engaged in a noble journey of inward self-discovery [*Innerlichkeit*]). It is this latter individual that Marx felt strongly compelled to defend (against capitalism), as did Weber (against bureaucratization). Both the American individual and the individualism of German Romanticism can be described as "heroic," owing to the concerted mobilization of great energy indispensable to each. Nonetheless, they differ radically in "direction": Romanticism's inward-looking orientation opposes American individualism's "world mastery." An orientation to a shaping and forming of "the world" on behalf of an ethical design and "standards" is apparent in the American case. On the other hand, this activity-oriented civic individualism must be distinguished clearly from the Nietzschean "superman" as well as German Romanticism's unique individual: it implies types of activity attainable by *all* rather than a tiny elite. Furthermore, it is characterized by a tempered and dispassionate (*nüchternes*) deportment and rigorous discipline. See Kalberg 2012, pp. 291–300.

14.   Following Bellah's civil religion argument (1970, pp. 168–192), many theorists endow the civic sphere thoroughly with ritual values and norms—and then comprehend declines in civic activity as resulting from their weakening. They understand this decline as especially worrisome because it implies to

them the same weakness of "socialization" mechanisms that Durkheim feared would lead to high rates of anomie. Hence, again following Durkheim, these theorists argue that *society* (its institutions, norms, civic associations, and mechanisms of solidarity) *must* remain firmly in place and strong. This linear approach, stemming from Tocqueville and Durkheim, stands far removed from Weber's (a) interpretive understanding sociology, (b) dynamic analyses rooted in symbiotic dualisms, and (c) stress on the historical sources of, and carrier groups for, a *particular* type of action: ethical action that strongly influences daily activity and, indeed, *contains* a civic component.

15.   Exactly *how* influential cannot be "measured," Weber would argue, in parallel with his position in respect to the "exact" influence of the Reformation on the development of modern capitalism: "[I] rate it *very* highly indeed. I have constantly and scrupulously reflected on this question, and am not bothered that no 'numerical' ratio exists for historical attribution here" (see Weber 2011b, p. 271).

16.   Weber also rejects the use of analogies (see Kalberg 1994, p. 83).

17.   Perhaps Weber's most illuminating example of this aspect of his methodology can be found in *The Protestant Ethic*. Here his opposition to all generalizing from a single case is clearly rendered. He states explicitly his rejection of the view that the "spirit of capitalism's" origin can be discovered *only* in ascetic Protestantism: "We shall not defend here [the] foolish and doctrinaire [thesis] in any form ... that the 'capitalist spirit' ... *could* have originated *only* as an expression of certain influences of the Reformation" (2011c, p. 108).

18.   Albeit the "specific cases" Weber investigates involve far larger themes than is typical in social science research today. Even the rise of a "Protestant ethic" in a particular epoch and among identifiable groups of believers constitutes, to him, an effort to address a specific development. See 2011c, pp. 178–179.

19.   Weber makes this general point further in the chapter on rulership in Part I of *Economy and Society*: "Hence, the kind of terminology and classification set forth ... has in no sense the aim—indeed, it could not have it—to be exhaustive or to confine the whole of historical reality in a rigid scheme" (1968, pp. 263–264).

20.   Weber here moves on to the large terrain familiar to us as "objectivity in the social sciences," a subject that has provoked intense commentary. For his classic support of the notion of "objectivity," see 1949, pp. 50–112; 1946d; see also, for a summary of the major issues, Kalberg 2011c, pp. 311–319.

The American Journey

Observations and Ramifications

I N THE SUMMER of 1904, Max Weber was invited to present a lecture in late September at the famous St. Louis Universal Exposition and Congress of Arts and Science. Accompanied by his wife, Marianne, he landed on American shores on August 30.

Their ship had steamed past the Statue of Liberty and the Webers disembarked in lower Manhattan into the noisy din of the New World's "spirit of capitalism." A hectic, two-month tour began. As apparent from Marianne's account, Weber threw himself into the social life of this "modern reality" and soaked up information from a vast diversity of sources. He listened well, told stories frequently, interacted in a leisurely manner with people from a wide variety of backgrounds, and posed questions incessantly.[1]

Weber's German travel companions remarked that his walking pace quickened. New York's dynamism and the "fantastic stream" of people in this colossus enraptured him. His interest was lively, and his curiosity insatiable, and he refused to countenance the stiff opprobrium of several of his German travel companions (see Rollman 1993, pp. 367–368, 372–374). Weber had become immersed, as he wrote to his mother, in a rough and ready, raw and untamed society at the vanguard of the modern world. He "wished to appreciate everything and to absorb as much of it as possible" (Marianne Weber 1975, p. 281; see pp. 280–283).[2] Ernst Troeltsch, the distinguished theologian and one of his traveling companions, conveys Weber's admiration of New York:

> Weber is splendid. He ... talks much and educates me without interruption in the most interesting way. It is of great benefit to see with him this country of businesses. He, too, learns continuously from what he sees and attempts to work it through. But since he thinks *aloud* while doing so, it helps me. (Rollman 1993, p. 368; see p. 372)

The New York visit lasted ten days. It included sightseeing throughout the teeming metropolis and intensive discussions with family friends, distant relatives, and many new acquaintances.[3] Weber's spirit had now become animated after a long period of depression. The peripatetic couple next journeyed north along the Hudson River to Niagara Falls and then on to Chicago.

In this city, which Marianne Weber described as "the crystallization of the American spirit" (Marianne Weber, p. 285), they attended a banquet at the University of Chicago and met with social reformers Jane Addams and Florence Kelley at Hull House. There ensued a lively discussion on, among many other topics, the opposition of capitalist entrepreneurs to workplace safety regulations and the negative impact of large-scale immigration on the strength of labor unions. Marianne described Kelley, the chief inspector of factories in Illinois from 1893 to 1897, as "by far the most outstanding figure" the Webers met in America (see Marianne Weber, p. 302; Rollmann 1993, pp. 369–370, 375–376; Scaff 2011, pp. 43–48).[4]

Mixing awe and revulsion in his letters, Weber depicted Chicago as a city of ethnic stratification. Here the "guts" of modern capitalism were on open display, especially in its stockyards:

> There is a mad pell-mell of nationalities: Up and down the streets the Greeks shine the Yankees' shoes for 5 cents. The Germans are their waiters, the Irish take care of their politics, and the Italians of their dirtiest ditch digging. With the exception of the better residential districts, the whole tremendous city—more extensive

than London!—is like a man whose skin has been peeled off and whose intestines are seen at work. (Max Weber in Marianne Weber, p. 286)

Everywhere one is struck by the tremendous intensity of work—most of all in the "stockyards" with their "ocean of blood," where several thousand cattle and pigs are slaughtered every day. From the moment when the unsuspecting bovine enters the slaughtering area, is hit by a hammer and collapses, whereupon it is immediately gripped by an iron clamp, is hoisted up, and starts on its journey, it is in constant motion—past ever-new workers who eviscerate and skin it, etc., but are always (in the rhythm of the work) tied to the machine that pulls the animal past them. One sees an absolutely incredible output in this atmosphere of steam, muck, blood, and hides in which I teetered about together with a "boy" who was giving me a guided tour for fifty cents, trying to keep from being buried in the filth. There one can follow a pig from the sty to the sausage and the can. (Max Weber in Marianne Weber, p. 287)

A "magnificent wildness," Marianne writes of Chicago, coexisted with a "modern reality" that "indifferently swallowed up everything individual." Yet "its gentle features ... bespoke a capacity for love as well as kindness, justice, and a tenacious desire for beauty and spirituality" (Marianne Weber, p. 287).[5]

Weber presented his paper, "Capitalism and Rural Society in Germany" (1946a), in St. Louis to a small audience.[6] His wife was relieved: his first public lecture in more than six years, she writes, was excellently delivered and well-received (Marianne Weber, pp. 290–291). On this occasion Weber renewed his acquaintance with W. E. B. Du Bois, the American sociologist and civil rights reformer who had attended his lectures in Berlin in the early 1890s. Several years later he would describe Du Bois as "the most important sociological scholar anywhere in the Southern States, with whom no white scholar can compare" (1973, p. 312).[7]

Weber then journeyed west by train alone into "Indian country."[8] He investigated in Oklahoma, mainly through interviews, the ongoing partition of the Native American land and witnessed how the juggernaut of American capitalism confronted directly, and conquered, the frontier:

> There were many … things [here] of burning interest to Weber … : the conquest of the wilderness by civilization, a developing city and the developing state of Oklahoma in an area that had until recently been reserved for the Indians…. Here it was still possible to observe the unarmed subjugation and absorption of an "inferior" race by a "superior," more intelligent one, the transformation of Indian tribal property into private property, and the conquest of the virgin forest by colonists. Weber stayed with a half-breed. He watched, listened, transformed himself into his surroundings, and thus everywhere penetrated to the heart of things. (Marianne Weber, p. 291)[9]

The informality and friendliness of Americans continued to impress the Webers, though also their sturdy individualism, mutual respect for one another, and "can-do" approach to even the most intractable problems. The "lightning speed" of capitalism's transformation of the prairie appeared to Weber incapable of losing momentum:

> [McAlester, Oklahoma] is a more "civilized" place than Chicago. It would be quite wrong to believe that one can behave as one wishes. In the conversations, which are, to be sure, quite brief, the courtesy lies in the tone and the bearing, and the humor is nothing short of delicious. Too bad, in a year this place will look like Oklahoma [City], that is, like any other American city. With almost lightning speed everything that stands in the way of capitalistic culture is being crushed. (Max Weber in Marianne Weber, p. 293)

The quest for the sources of American life's fast pulse moved next to New Orleans. The Webers observed black-white relations here firsthand. Max would recall later, at a conference in Germany in 1911, his experiences and observations to support arguments against those who proclaimed the superiority of "the European race" (see 1971a; 1973; 2005, pp. 306–313; Winter 2004).

The Webers next visited Tuskegee Institute in Alabama.[10] An emotional tour of the black college followed: "What they found [here] probably moved them more than anything else on their trip. The great national problem of all American life, the showdown between the white race and the former slaves, could here be grasped at its roots" (Marianne Weber, p. 295).[11] To Weber, "the Americans are a wonderful people, and only the Negro question and the terrible immigration constitute the big black clouds" (Max Weber in Marianne Weber, p. 302). His general assessment would be soon offered in a letter to Du Bois: "I am absolutely convinced that the color line-problem will be the paramount problem of the time to come, here and everywhere in the world."[12] Weber's hope to return to the South "as soon as possible" remained unfulfilled.

Distant relatives at the edge of the Blue Ridge Mountains in Mt. Airy, North Carolina, were then visited for several days. While observing an adult baptism ceremony, one of Weber's cousins scoffed when a young acquaintance stepped forward. Upon inquiry, the candidate's motives were revealed as suspect: he wished to open a new business in the neighborhood, Weber's cousin explained. Church membership, which was allowed only after scrutiny of the candidate's "good character," would offer solid evidence of his trustworthiness—and merchants who were known to offer fair deals and just prices would be preferred throughout the community over others (see Weber 2011d, pp. 209–212).[13]

Brief visits to Washington, Baltimore, and Philadelphia ensued. Along the way, the visitors attended Quaker, Presbyterian, Methodist, white Baptist, black Baptist, and Christian Science services (Marianne Weber, pp. 288–289, 300–301).[14] Marianne's relatives hosted the travelers in a northern suburb of Boston in a modest home on a quiet street.[15] They explored the city and attended the Harvard-Yale game (see Marianne Weber, p. 301).[16] Weber presumably met with Harvard's distinguished psychologist William James. "Worlds by themselves," America's colleges impressed the sojourners,[17] who perceived here "the tradition of the Pilgrim fathers" (Marianne Weber, pp. 133, 301, 288).

The whole magic of youthful memories attaches solely to this period. An abundance of sports, attractive forms of social life, infinite intellectual stimulation, and lasting friendship are the returns, and above all the education includes far more habituation to work than there is among our students. (Max Weber in Marianne Weber, p. 288)

The tradition of the Pilgrim fathers ... still bound the young men to the ideal of chastity, prohibited smutty stories, and instilled into them a measure of chivalry toward women which was unknown to the average German of the day. (Marianne Weber, p. 288)

After an evening attending a play in Yiddish in a Jewish neighborhood in New York, the Webers departed for Germany on the 19th of November.

Weber had been an avid international traveler since his teenage years.[18] The train grid in Europe became comprehensive during his lifetime, and his many journeys took him across the expanse of the continent from southern Italy to northern Scotland. However, the United States left an indelible mark. He referred often in later years in public lectures and writings to personal observations.[19]

Most of Weber's German colleagues were convinced that American capitalism threatened the ethical integrity of individuals, exploited workers systematically, and destroyed viable social ties, leaving people adrift and "atomized."[20] Weber, on the other hand, for the most part embraced the United States, absorbed its heterogeneity, and perceived in this nation firm ethical standards, an openness, and a rigorous sense of purpose lacking in Europe: "For there was a youthfully fresh, confident energy, a force for good that was just as powerful as the evil forces" (Marianne Weber, p. 302).[21] Indeed, he wished to confront stereotypes widespread in Germany.[22] However, he foresaw, as discussed previously (see Chapter 5), a longer-term diminution of its economic growth and a gradual bureaucratization of its political parties, economic organizations, and civil service. This future "Europeanization" of the United States implied less egalitarianism, more rigid social hierarchies, and less dynamism, he feared.

This eleven-week journey significantly influenced not only Weber's analysis of the American political culture, but also his various writings on the sociology of religion, political leadership, bureaucracies, democracy, status groups, stratification in general, and race and ethnicity. Moreover, he gained a clearer understanding of how past developments in the realm of religion lived on and penetrated into, in secularized and quasi-secularized forms, the present. Finally, he comprehended with greater insight the ways in which modern industrial and urbanized societies differ. Surely his understanding of the particularity—and weaknesses—of the German political and economic cultures was enhanced as a consequence of knowledge acquired during this journey.[23]

Notes

1. Much of this section rests on Marianne Weber's discussion of the journey. See 1975, pp. 279–304; see also the interesting studies by Roth 1985, 2005a, 2005b; Rollman 1993; Scaff 1998, 2005; and Mommsen 1974, 1998, 2000. The definitive work now on Weber's journey is the excellent work by Scaff 2011.

2. Quotations are from Marianne Weber unless otherwise noted.

3. On the New York City visit, and in particular its connections to Weber's extended family, see Roth 2001, 2005a, 2005b.

4. Kelley became the American editor of the journal Weber coedited, *Archiv für Sozialwissenschaft und Sozialpolitik*.

5. For a fine portrait of the period of residence in Chicago, see Scaff 2011, pp. 40–53.

6. This lecture (1946a) is summarized by Scaff (see 2011, pp. 60–64). For an abridged version, see Weber 2005, pp. 142–146. On the conference generally, see Rollman 1993; Scaff 2011, pp. 60–64; and Roth 1987, pp. 175–182.

7. Weber encouraged Du Bois to write an article for his journal. His attempt to arrange the translation into German and publication of the "splendid work" by Du Bois, *The Souls of Black Folk* (2003), failed, despite Weber's plan "to write a short introduction about [the] Negro question and literature." He had also intended to write an article on "the recent publications [on] the race problem in America." See Weber's letter in English to Du Bois (Aptheker 1973, p. 106). See also Scaff 1998; 2011, pp. 102–108. On Weber's views on race, see 1971a; 1973; 2005, pp. 297–314; Manasse 1947; Peukert 1989; Scaff 1998, pp. 69–73; 2011, pp. 112–116; Winter 2004; Kalberg 2005.

8. Marianne Weber stayed in St. Louis. Traveling by train, they later met, on the way to New Orleans, in Memphis.

9. See the fascinating description of this aspect of Weber's journey by Scaff 2005, pp. 85–109; 2011, pp. 73–97.

10. Its president, Booker T. Washington, was unfortunately traveling at the time of the visit. Weber was familiar with Washington's major writings, and they later corresponded. See Scaff 1998, pp. 69–70; 2011, pp. 108–112.

11. "The whites are bleeding to death because of this separation [in the South] intended as 'racial protection,' and the only enthusiasm in the South may be found among [the often nine-tenths white] Negro upper class; among the whites there is only random, knee-jerk hatred of the Yankees" (Max Weber in Marianne Weber 1975, p. 296; translation altered).

12. Letter to Du Bois, November 17, 1904 (quoted in Scaff 2011, p. 100). As Scaff notes, this was the position Du Bois had earlier articulated. Weber had read the major works of Du Bois (see Scaff 1998, pp. 69–71; 2011, pp. 100–108).

13. Relatives who recalled Weber's visit to North Carolina were interviewed. See Keeter 1981. Marianne's general comment appears on the mark: "Unexpectedly Weber even here acquired illustrative material for his work: old and new forms of the social stratification of democratic society. In an elemental form he saw the life-forming effect of religious sects . . ." (Marianne Weber, p. 298; see also Weber's letter cited at pp. 288–289).

14. Weber comments in a long letter in detail on the Christian Science service. See Scaff 1998, pp. 67–68; 2011, pp. 164–168.

15. Wyoming, now Malden, Massachusetts.

16. With their hosts, the Webers sat in a carriage in the end zone. However, boredom set in, and they left at halftime.

17. Max briefly visited libraries and archives at Columbia, Harvard, and Haverford College. He visited nearly all the major East Coast universities, including the campuses of Yale, Johns Hopkins, Brown, and Harvard. He "sometimes attended classes in order to observe American teaching methods" (Marianne Weber, p. 288). See Scaff 2011, pp. 141–142, 161.

18. On the extremely cosmopolitan character of Weber's far-flung family, see Roth 2001, 2005b.

19. On Weber's views of the United States generally, see Mommsen 1974; Roth 1985, 2005a, 2005b; Scaff 1998, 2011; Berger 1971; and Rollman 1993. On the influence on the young Weber of American Unitarianism and the Social Gospel movement, see Roth 1997. On Weber's youthful readings on the United States, see Scaff 2005, pp. 80–81; 2011, p. 12; Roth 2005b. Weber's interest in America stretches back to his mid-teen years (see Weber 1936, p. 29).

20. The letters home of Weber's friend and travel companion in New York, Werner Sombart, lamented "this dreadful cultural hell" and the "chamber of horrors of capitalism" (Lenger 1994, pp. 148–149).

21. This sentence is from Marianne Weber.

22. Nonetheless, Weber also repeatedly depicted the widespread corruption in the "machine politics" of large American cities. See 1968, p. 1401; 1946b, pp. 107–111; Marianne Weber, p. 302. He also referred critically to its widespread consumerism. See Chapter 5, pp. 78–80.

23. Weber's notion of "plebiscitary democracy," which he wished to introduce into Germany and which contrasted European-style political parties rooted in ideology with American-style parties anchored in the appeal of individual leaders, appears to be taken directly from the American model.

APPENDIX II

The Protestant Ethic and the Spirit of Capitalism
A Brief Summary

PUBLISHED ORIGINALLY AS two long articles in 1904 and 1905 in the *Archiv für Sozialwissenschaft und Sozialpolitik*, Max Weber's classic, *The Protestant Ethic and the Spirit of Capitalism* (*PE*; 2011b), is one of the most enduring and widely read volumes in modern social science. A brief review of its major points will assist understanding of Weber's analysis of the American political culture.[1]

PE investigated whether the "Protestant ethic" found among seventeenth-century Puritans (Calvinists, Methodists, Baptists, Mennonites, and Quakers) "*co*-participated" in giving birth to a driving force Weber saw as contributing to the rise of the industrial West: a secular "spirit of capitalism." Adherents of this "modern economic ethic" viewed work as a systematic endeavor, he argued, namely, as a *calling* (*Beruf*). Characteristic was a rigorous—"an ascetic"—organization of occupational life according to a set of values, a methodical and dutiful striving for profit and wealth, and a systematic reinvestment of money rather than its enjoyment. The deeply rooted religious world of the sixteenth and seventeenth centuries must be briefly noted if Weber's argument is to be understood.

The "Spiritual Foundation"

The doctrine of Predestination anchors his argument in *PE*. According to John Calvin (1509–1564), a Swiss theologian, an omniscient and omnipotent God of the Old Testament has determined that only a chosen few will be reborn into heaven. Good works or ethical behavior can never influence His decisions, nor can mere mortals understand His motives. Unbearable anxiety and fatalism for the faithful were the consequence of this doctrine, Weber noted. However, revisions were undertaken in the later sixteenth and early seventeenth centuries by "Puritan divines," a group of ministers, theologians, and lay believers in England led by Richard Baxter (1615–1691). Herein lies the source of the Protestant ethic, Weber maintains. His analysis at this point can be seen to divide into two stages.

First, following Calvin, the Puritans saw their task in this short life in unequivocal terms: to construct on earth a Kingdom that would extoll His glory and majesty—that is, a Kingdom of wealth and abundance. Hence, work, as a means of constructing this Kingdom, was awarded with a "psychological premium," "commanded to all," and elevated by the sincere devout to the forefront of life. In addition, labor must involve a systematic element, the divines held; it must be performed *in a calling*. Moreover, by taming base wants and desires, systematic labor assists concentration on God and His plan. It also dispels the overwhelming doubt, anxiety, and sense of moral unworthiness caused by the doctrine of Predestination. In this manner this *ascetic Protestantism* bestowed clear premiums on constant labor and the search for riches. Both activities now lost their exclusively utilitarian meaning and became providential.

Although influential, this sanctification failed to fully overcome the long-standing ethos rooted in medieval Catholicism. According to this "traditional economic ethic," labor was understood as a necessary evil, and profit was seldom earned honestly. If a banishment of this frame of mind (*Gesinnung*) were to occur, work and wealth had to acquire an even more comprehensive sanctification, *PE* held. After all, this ethic had been uprooted only rarely. Entrepreneurial astuteness and "business savvy," all intelligent modes of making one's way in the world (*Lebensklugheit*), and even charismatic adventure capitalists had failed to bring about its weakening (2011c, pp. 79, 83–84). Furthermore, the all-important "certainty of salvation" (*certitudo salutis*) question to anxious believers—"am I among the saved?"—had not yet been answered adequately. In this regard, the second stage of Weber's analysis proves crucial.

Despite the Predestination decree, Baxter and other Puritan divines concluded that *signs* from God of the believer's salvation status could be discovered. Above all, the Deity's favor seemed apparent if the devout demonstrated a capacity, as required by their vocational calling, either to labor systematically or to remain focused on the onerous task of acquiring wealth. Indeed, the faithful convinced themselves that their strength and discipline to do so, as well as their deep devotion and righteous conduct, came from God: His energy was "operating within." Furthermore, surely in His cosmos, nothing occurred by chance: those believers who, by dint of methodical work, managed to acquire great wealth, understood their good fortune as a consequence of God's hand—and the devout could convince themselves that He would assist *only* the predestined. Systematic work, as well as the acquisition of profit and great wealth, became "evidence" of one's favorable salvation status.

Now awarded psychological premiums in an even more intense manner, constant labor and the possession of riches became viewed by the faithful as *testifying* to their salvation. They offered literal proof (*Bewährung*) to believers of redemption. As anxiety declined, the bleak Puritan became transformed into a disciplined "tool" of God's will, proudly engaged in the large task of building His glorious Kingdom on earth.

According to Weber, this *methodical-rational* organization of life and *inner-worldly asceticism*—a "Protestant ethic"—distinguished the "Puritan style of life." The devout now focused their energies and conduct in a comprehensive manner on God's will, restricted consumption, reinvested profits, banished the traditional economic ethic, and placed work at the center of life. Extreme loyalty to His grand design marked the faithful, as did cognizance that riches emanated from the hand of this omnipotent Deity and thus belonged exclusively to Him and His Kingdom. Wealth *must* be, on His behalf and for His community, invested instead of enjoyed.

Simultaneously, the image of those engaged in business and oriented to profit changed. Rather than viewed as calculating, greedy, and self-interested, as had been the case since antiquity, capitalists were now perceived as honest employers of good character sincerely engaged in a noble project given by God. The halo of religion—a "spiritual founda-tion"—surrounded their activities, and hence the understanding of the production and exchange of goods as involving exclusively utilitarian calculations and clever business procedures must be abandoned, Weber contends. Specialists in vocations—a new "human being" (*Menschentyp*) engaged in a calling—now embarked upon the stage of Western history.

He insists that the Puritan anchoring of methodical orientations toward work, wealth, and profit in the major question for believers—"am I among the saved?"—proved significant. The concerted bestowing of religion-based psychological rewards on vocational labor was alone endowed with the capacity to uproot the traditional economic ethic. The tenacity and "lasting resilience" (2011c, p. 91) of this *coherent group* of persons—Puritan employers and workers—must be acknowl-edged, he argues. The "internally binding" set of religious values that motivated work "from within," and the search for material success, introduced the life "organized around ethical principles." This forceful patterning of action confronted directly the traditional economic ethic. To Weber, the manifold ethical dimension that penetrated the Puritan's economic activity constituted a "revolutionary" force against this ethic (2011c, pp. 89, 134–135). It also called forth a spirit of capitalism.

From the Protestant Ethic to the Spirit of Capitalism

Carried by churches and sects, the Protestant ethic spread throughout many New England, Dutch, and English communities in the seven-teenth century. Disciplined, hard labor in a calling marked a person as among the chosen, as did the wealth that followed from a steadfast adherence to Puritan values. This ethos was cultivated in entire regions in Benjamin Franklin's era one century later. However, its religion-based, ethical component had become weaker with this expansion and became transformed—namely, into an "ethos with a utilitarian accent" (2011c, pp. 79, 173, 176–178).

Weber refers to this ethos as the spirit of capitalism: a configuration of values that implied the individual's duty to view work as an end in itself, to labor systematically in a calling, to increase capital, to earn money perpetually (while avoiding enjoyment of it), and to comprehend material wealth as a manifestation of "competence and proficiency in a vocational calling" (2011c, p. 81). Adherents to this mode of organizing life, rather than perceived by others as among the saved, were believed to be community-oriented citizens of good moral character. Immediately recognizable, their stalwart demeanor no longer served to testify to firm belief and membership among the elect; it indicated instead respectability, dignity, honesty, and self-confidence.[2]

Franklin represented this "spirit" in *PE*. Business astuteness, utilitarian calculations, and greed fail to account for the *origin* of his disciplined life, Weber contends; legacies of ascetic Protestantism contributed substantially. Indeed, such an interpretation is confirmed by the presence of an ethical element in Franklin's manner of organizing and directing his life, Weber holds (2011c, pp. 79–81). A conundrum, however, here appears. How had the ethical dimension in the Protestant ethic, now shorn of its foundational salvation quest and "in but not of" the world components, survived into Franklin's era?

Long before the religious roots of ethical action had become weakened, the Puritans' ethical values had expanded beyond their original social carriers—ascetic Protestant churches and sects—to another carrier organization: Protestant families. For this reason, these values remained central in childhood socialization *even* as Colonial America experienced a gradual loosening of the all-encompassing influence of these congregations. Parents taught children to set goals and organize their lives methodically, to be self-reliant and shape their own destinies as individuals, to behave in accord with ethical standards, and to work diligently. They encouraged their offspring to pursue careers in business and see virtue in capitalism's open markets, to seek material success, to become upwardly mobile, to live modestly and frugally, to reinvest their wealth, to look toward the future and the "opportunities" it offers, and to budget their time wisely—just as Franklin had admonished in his writings (2011c, pp. 77–78). Families also stressed ascetic personal habits, hard competition, and the importance of honesty and fair play in business transactions. Through intimate, personal relationships,[3] children were socialized to conduct themselves in a restrained, dispassionate manner—and to do so by reference to a configuration of ethical values.

In this way, action oriented toward values originally carried by ascetic Protestant sects and churches endured long after the weakening of these religious organizations. An orientation toward ethical action became cultivated also in community organizations, including schools. Protestantism's "sect spirit," now routinized into maxims, community norms, a particular demeanor, and familiar customs and traditions, continued to influence new generations; they remained integral in Franklin's America (see 2011a, pp. 227–232; see Nelson 1973, pp. 98–99, 106–108). Yet the ancestry of this spirit of capitalism was not "this-worldly" but "other-worldly," Weber contends. The Protestant ethic constituted its predecessor: "The Puritan's sincerity of belief must have been the most powerful lever conceivable working to expand the life outlook that we are here designating as the spirit of capitalism" (2011c, p. 170):

> Our analysis should have demonstrated that one of the constitutive components of the modern capitalist spirit and, moreover, generally of modern civilization, was the rational organization of life on the basis of the *idea of the calling*. It was born out of the spirit of *Christian asceticism*. (2011c, p. 176; emphasis in original)

Having illustrated "the way in which 'ideas' become generally effective in history" (2011c, p. 107), *PE* now reaches its conclusion. Weber has traced the lineage of the spirit of capitalism and discovered significant nonutilitarian, nonpolitical, and noneconomic roots. A Protestant ethic had, *PE* affirms, "*co*-participated" in the formation of the spirit of capitalism (2011c, p. 108).[4] The realm of values and ideas had played a prominent causal role.

The "Mechanical" Foundations

PE's last pages leap across the centuries in order briefly to survey a new theme: the "cosmos" of modern capitalism. In broad strokes and unforgettable passages, Weber briefly explores the fate today of "this-worldly" directed action and the life organized methodically by reference to a constellation of ethical values. The question of how we *can* live under modern capitalism preoccupied him for his entire life.

Firmly entrenched after the massive industrialization of the nineteenth century, "victorious capitalism" now sustains itself on the basis of *means-end rational* action alone, Weber argues. In this urban and bureaucratic milieu, neither Franklin's spirit nor the Protestant ethic's asceticism endows methodical work with subjective meaning. Sheer utilitarian calculations move to the forefront as these value configurations, so significant at the birth of modern capitalism, collapse and fade (2011c, pp. 175–176). Today, modern capitalism unfolds on the basis of an inescapable network of pragmatic necessities.

Whether employees or entrepreneurs, people born into this "powerful cosmos" are coerced to adapt to its market-based, functional exchanges in order to survive. The motivation to work in this "steel-hard casing" (*stahlhartes Gehäuse*) involves a mixture of constraint and means-end rational action. A "mechanical foundation" anchors our era. Modern capitalism—this "grinding mechanism"—will "[determine the style of life of all born into it] ... with overwhelming force, and perhaps it will continue to do so until the last ton of fossil fuel has burnt to ashes" (2011c, p. 177).[5]

This acknowledgment of his brief commentary upon capitalist societies today reveals Weber's analysis in *PE* as characterized by four discrete stages (see the chart on page 134).

In sum, a dynamic tapestry characterizes the *PE* analysis. Despite regular indictments, the Weber thesis survives to this day and must be confronted by scholars seeking to understand the rise of modern capitalism in the West. By calling attention to the important historical roles played by both a Protestant ethic and a spirit of capitalism, *PE* questions all those theories that explain the rise of the modern world exclusively by reference to utilitarian activity (for example, rational choice theory) or structural transformations (whether of Marxian or Durkheimian lineage). The varying *subjective meaning* of persons in demarcated groups proved central to Weber, as did the *other*-worldly, *value*-oriented ancestry of the modern world. The Puritan's asceticism originated from his life "*in* but not *of*" the world.

The Protestant Ethic and the Spirit of Capitalism: Stages of Weber's Analysis

	Period	Organization	Type of Action	Devout
I. **Calvin**: Fatalism follows from Predestination Doctrine	16th C.	small sects	value-rational	yes
II. **Baxter**: The Protestant Ethic	16th–17th C.	churches and sects	value-rational (methodical worldly activity)	yes
III. **Franklin**: The spirit of capitalism	18th C.	communities	value-rational (methodical worldly activity)	no
IV. The "**specialist**": Modern capitalism as a "cosmos"	20th C.	industrial society	means-end rational	no

elective ‹---› affinity

PE must be comprehended as the father of all schools of sociological thought that, in seeking to explain long-range social change, explicitly attend to cultural forces. It must be further understood as declaring emphatically that the past is interwoven with, and influences, the present. Finally, in an age of universalizing globalization, *PE* conveys the causal significance of the indigenous cultural makeup inevitably manifest when a nation embarks upon economic modernization. Weber admonished social scientists generally to take account of religion-based, background contexts for social change.

Notes

1. This overview offers a succinct summary of "the Weber thesis." It provides the background context to Chapters 1 and 2. For a more detailed discussion, see Kalberg 2011a; 2011c, pp. 321–330.

2. The origins of the American emphasis on honesty and candor toward all as a central aspect of "good character," to be manifested both in personal conduct and even in the political realm (as an ideal for political activists), must be sought here. For the Puritan, righteous conduct that testified to one's elect status emanated ultimately from God's strength *within* the believer—and He could not be other than candid. For the same reason, persons speaking to Puritans would not dare speak dishonestly.

3. Weber argues that the teaching of *ethical* values, if it is to occur, necessarily involves a strong personal bond. See, for example, 1927, pp. 357–358; 1946c, p. 331; 1968, pp. 346, 600, 1186–1187; 2005, pp. 251–254.

4. That Weber acknowledges the existence of other origins of this spirit is apparent. See 2011c, pp. 108, 399–400, note 142.

5. This theme has been visited at various points throughout this volume.

Glossary

This list includes (a) terms central to the main themes of this volume and (b) technical terms at the foundation of Weber's sociology. Italics indicate a cross-reference to another entry in this Glossary.

American spectrum. In the twenty-first century, pendulum movements occur across Weberian (see Chapter 5) and complementary (see Chapter 6) models.

ascetic Protestantism (Puritanism). This generic term refers to the Calvinist, Pietist, Methodist, Quaker, Baptist, and Mennonite *churches* and *sects*. Weber compares and contrasts the vocational ethics of these faiths to each other and to those of Lutheran Protestantism and Catholicism. All Puritans organized their lives around work and a morally rigorous asceticism—hence, Puritanism provides a consistent foundation for the idea of a vocational *calling*, Weber argues. Remarkably, because oriented to salvation in the next life rather than this-worldly goods or interests, the intense activity of Puritans was *in* the world but not *of* the world. He discovers one clear source of a *spirit of capitalism* in their teachings and practices.

asceticism. An extreme taming, channeling, sublimating, and organizing of the believer's spontaneous human drives and wants (the *status naturae*) by a set of values. Asceticism grounded in values a "methodical-rational organization of life" in two "directions": *in* the world (the "this-worldly asceticism" of the ascetic Protestants) and *outside* the world (the "other-worldly asceticism" of monks in monasteries).

calling (*Beruf*). Originally denoted a task given by God; hence, it must be honored and performed diligently. The calling introduced a demarcated and respected realm of work into the Protestant believer's life in the sixteenth and seventeenth centuries in the West. It continues to exist today, albeit in secularized form, namely, as "service" to a profession or to a community.

carriers. See *social carriers*.

church. Persons are "born into" a church and, hence, are obligatory members. Unlike a *sect*, a church "lets grace shine over the righteous and unrighteous alike." See *sect*.

civic association. Prominent in the American nineteenth century as community service organizations (for example, the Rotary, Lions, and Kiwanis clubs). Their sociological precursors are found in the eighteenth-century Protestant *sects*, Weber maintains. As in these groups, membership, which resulted from a favorable vote, conferred status and respectability. Their widespread proliferation led Weber to reject the common view of American society in Europe: as a *sandpile* of unconnected individuals.

civic individualism (practical-ethical individualism). A nineteenth-century legacy of Puritanism. Implies an orientation by Americans to a set of values articulated by a *civic sphere*. These values are understood to be ethical—that is, they set standards and ideals in reference to which persons feel an obligation. Hence, civic individualism involves a posture of activism in reference to values. Weber sees this type of individualism as threatened in the twentieth century by *practical-rational* individualism.

civic sphere. A set of values separate from the private realm that sets community standards toward which citizens are sincerely oriented as ideals.

ethical action. Rooted in values and involving an obligatory element that contains the potential strongly to direct action. Weber sees ethical action as weakened and circumscribed in the modern era to the extent that *practical* and *formal rationality* expand.

formal rationality. Omnipresent in modern capitalism, modern law, bureaucratic authority, and the modern state, this type of rationality implies decision making "without regard to persons"; that is, by reference to sets of universally applied rules, laws, statutes, and regulations.

frame of mind (*Gesinnung*). The temperament or disposition specific to the *subjective* meaning common in a group of people. It can be conceptualized by the formation of an *ideal type*, Weber contends, that highlights essential features, for example, of Calvinists, Catholics, Lutherans, feudal aristocrats, old commerce-oriented distinguished (patrician) families, and persons in the middle class. In some groups the frame of mind may be more influenced by values (and even ethical values, as in religious groups); in others it may be more influenced by interests or traditions (customs and conventions).

"grinding mechanism." See *steel-hard casing*.

"hold your own." The *ascetic Protestant* believer, even in groups that monitor strictly his behavior, is still responsible directly to God. A priest, serving as an intermediary, is absent, and the faithful must testify (*sich bewähren*) to their own salvation through conduct. Despite temptation, the devout must hold their own, in respect to His commandments.

ideal type. Weber's major methodological tool. This heuristic concept seeks to capture, by accentuating that which is characteristic from the point of view of the researcher's theme, the essential *subjective meaning* in a group (such as the economic ethics of persons affiliated with different religions). Once formed, ideal types serve as standards against which particular empirical cases can be "measured" and then defined. They are also central in establishing causality. Ideal types constitute Weber's level of analysis rather than historical narrative, rational choices, or global concepts (society, modernization).

interpretive understanding (*Verstehen*; see *subjective meaning*). This is the term Weber uses to describe his methodology. He wishes to understand the patterned actions of people in demarcated groups by reconstructing the milieu of values, traditions, interests, and emotions (see *social action*) within which they live, and thereby to comprehend how their subjective meaning is formulated.

meaningful action. See *social action*.

new symbiotic dualism. See *symbiotic dualism*.

practical-ethical individualism. See *civic individualism*.

practical rationality (practical rationalism; practical-rational individualism). The random flow of daily interests is here central, and the individual's adaptation—through means-end rational calculations—to them. Contrasts directly to ethical action, according to which the random flow of interests is confronted and ordered by a patterned orientation of action to values.

Predestination (doctrine of). Prominent especially among Calvinists. God has willed a few to be saved; most are condemned. His reasons are unknowable and no human activity can change one's "predestination status." The logical consequence of belief in this doctrine was fatalism and despair among the devout. Revisions by theologians and ministers ("Puritan divines") led to the *Protestant ethic*.

Protestant ethic. A source of the *spirit of capitalism*. Sixteenth- and seventeenth-century interpretations of the Calvinist *doctrine of Predestination* eventually led to a situation in which believers could experience "psychological rewards" vis-à-vis their salvation status once they successfully oriented their action to methodical work, economic competition, profit, and the attainment of wealth.

Protestant sects (see *sect*). Members were "balloted" in on the basis of "good moral character," and their behavior was then monitored strictly. The high prestige of sects in their communities was retained in the process. Remarkably, *both* high conformity pressures *and* high pressure to act as an individual responsible to God's decrees coexisted in this organization.

providential (sanctified). Rendering with religious (salvation) significance an activity heretofore purely utilitarian (work, wealth, and profit, for example).

psychological reward (*psychologische Prämien*). Through belief and the practice of religion, "salvation premiums" are awarded by *ascetic* Protestants to particular activities (such as the accumulation of wealth or the organization of life in accord with God's laws), thereby assisting the devout, as long as they execute these activities, to more easily convince themselves of their membership among the saved.

Puritans. See *ascetic Protestantism.*

rational. A systematic, rigorous, disciplined element to action.

rationalization of action. A systematization of action, conceivably to the point of a "methodical-rational" organization of life grounded in a comprehensive orientation to values. Ascetic Protestant believers "rationalized" their activities in the most rigorous fashion.

routinization. The patterned action of persons in groups can be captured, according to Weber, by reference to four types of *social action.* If action originally oriented toward values later becomes calculating and exclusively means-end rational, it has become "routinized."

sanctified. See *providential.*

sandpile. American society, Weber contends, is not a "sandpile" of atomized individuals—that is, persons without substantive relationships. Rather, a "tremendous flood of *civic* and social associations from the beginning penetrated all corners of American life," pulling individuals securely into groups.

sect. As opposed to a church, an exclusive and tightly knit group that admits new members only once specific moral criteria have been fulfilled. Hence, all members are "certified" as of "good character." A monitoring of behavior to ensure compliance with high ethical standards is intense. See *church.*

social action (meaningful action). Weber's sociology seeks "to offer an interpretive understanding of social action." Unlike "reactive" or "imitative" action, social action implies a subjectively meaningful component that "takes account of the behavior of others." This aspect can be understood by the researcher. Weber identifies (as ideal types) four "types of social action": affectual, traditional, means-end rational, and value-rational. Among other major goals, his *Economy and Society* seeks to chart out the social contexts that call forth meaningful action in a variety of societal domains (for example, the economy, religion, law, and authority arenas).

social carriers (*Träger*). Patterned social action oriented to values, traditions, interests, emotions, and ideas becomes important as a causal force, according to Weber, when "carried" by demarcated and influential groups (classes, status groups, organizations). He wishes to know in *The Protestant Ethic* volume what groups carried specific types of vocational ethics. A central concept in his sociology.

spirit of capitalism (modern, rational economic ethic). Represented by Benjamin Franklin, this spirit constitutes a secularized legacy of the *Protestant ethic*, to which it is related in an "elective affinity" relationship. It refers to a methodical orientation toward profit and competition, work "as an absolute end in itself," and a perceived duty to increase one's wealth (yet the avoidance of its enjoyment). Weber insists that its origin cannot be located in utilitarian economic activity; rather, a set of religious values and the quest among *ascetic Protestant* believers for certainty of their salvation constitutes the source of this *frame of mind*. An important causal factor, Weber argued that this "spirit" played a role at the birth of modern capitalism.

steel-hard casing ("iron cage"; *stahlhartes Gehäuse*). Once "in the saddle," modern capitalism no longer requires a *spirit of capitalism* as a supporting pillar. Rather, this "grinding mechanism" now sustains itself entirely on the basis of adherence to the laws of the market. Impersonal calculation, instrumental rationality, and mechanisms to maximize efficient production characterize this steel-hard casing. The widespread bureaucratization that accompanies modern capitalism exacerbates the impersonal and harsh character of the steel-hard casing.

subjective meaning. Weber's sociology never aspires to establish that which is objectively valid. Rather, it seeks to understand the subjective meaningfulness of particular patterned action by persons in specific groups (e.g., churches, sects, bureaucracies, status groups, etc.). Throughout his sociology, Weber seeks to comprehend how persons lend their behavior meaning (no matter how odd it may appear to the observer). He wishes in *The Protestant Ethic* volume, for example, to understand why, for ascetic Protestants, continuous hard work constitutes a subjectively meaningful endeavor. *Ideal types* capture subjective meaning.

symbiotic dualism. Weber sees an unusual synthesis in the American political culture—namely, an activity-oriented, *world-mastery* individualism became juxtaposed with an orientation of persons to the values of a viable *civic sphere*. A mutually sustaining relationship congealed. He discovers the original manifestation of this dualism in seventeenth- and eighteenth-century Puritan sects (see Chapters 1 and 2) and its later—secular—manifestation in nineteenth-century civic associations (a *new symbiotic dualism*; see Chapter 3).

testify before people (see *sect*; *Protestant sects*). "Qualities of a certain kind" were indispensable to become a *sect* member, and devout conduct must be maintained continuously. Owing to the sect's close monitoring of behavior, Weber argues, the faithful were required to "*hold their own before people*" in order to sustain self-esteem and respectability. He saw "no stronger means of breeding traits than through the necessity of holding one's own" in the "circle of one's associates."

utilitarian adaptation to the world. The orientation of life to the pragmatic morality of the world rather than a surpassing of this morality on the basis of a rigorous orientation to God's laws and a striving for salvation.

value-rational action (motives). One of Weber's "four types of *social action*," this term implies that people may orient their conduct to values to a significant extent, indeed even to the degree that values become obligatory, or "binding." He often contrasts this type of meaningful action to "means-end rational action."

vocational calling. See *calling*.

world-mastery. The *frame of mind* of Puritan believers. They seek to "master" worldly obstacles, randomness, and injustice in order to create on earth an orderly, just, and affluent Kingdom of God. In accord with their Deity's commandments, such a Kingdom will glorify His majesty. Weber sees here an activist and initiative-taking posture. The *spirit of capitalism* constitutes its secular manifestation.

Bibliography

Abbott, Andrew. 1983. "Professional Ethics." *American Journal of Sociology* 88: 855–885.

Abel, Richard I. 1985. "Comparative Sociology of Legal Professions: An Exploratory Essay." *American Bar Foundation Research Journal* 10: 1–79.

———. 1986. "The Transformation of the American Legal Profession." *Law and Society Review* 20: 7–17.

Abel, Richard I., and Philip S. C. Lewis, eds. 1989. *Lawyers in Society in Comparative Theories*. Berkeley: University of California Press.

Almond, Gabriel, and Sidney Verba. 1963. *The Civic Culture*. Boston, MA: Little Brown.

Aptheker, Herbert, ed. 1973. *The Correspondence of W. E. B. Du Bois* (vol. 1, 1877–1934). Amherst: University of Massachusetts Press.

Arato, Andrew, and Eike Gebhardt, eds. 1982. *The Essential Frankfurt School Reader*. New York: Continuum.

Bailyn, Bernard. 1967. *The Ideological Origins of the American Revolution*. Cambridge, MA: Belknap/Harvard.

Barber, Bernard. 1978–1979. "Control and Responsibility in the Powerful Professions." *Political Science Quarterly* 93: 599–615.

Barlett, Donald L., and James B. Steele. 2012. *The Betrayal of the American Dream*. Washington, DC: Public Affairs.

Bell, Daniel. 1996. *The Cultural Contradictions of Capitalism*. New York: Basic Books.

Bellah, Robert. 1970. *Beyond Belief*. New York: Harper and Row.

———. 1975. *The Broken Covenant*. Chicago: University of Chicago Press.

———. 1992. *The Good Society*. Berkeley: University of California Press.

Bellah, Robert, Richard Madsen, William M. Sullivan, Ann Swidler, and Steven M. Tipton. 1985. *Habits of the Heart*. Berkeley: University of California Press.

Bendix, Reinhard. 1978. *Kings or People*. Berkeley: University of California Press.

Bendix, Reinhard, and Guenther Roth. 1971. *Scholarship and Partisanship*. Berkeley: University of California Press.

Berger, Stephen D. 1971. "The Sects and the Breakthrough into the Modern World." *Sociological Quarterly* 12 (Autumn): 486–499.

Berghahn, Volker. 2005. *Imperial Germany: Economy, Society, Culture, and Politics*. New York: Berghahn Books.

Brint, Stephen. 1994. *In an Age of Experts*. Princeton, NJ: Princeton University Press.

Bronner, Stephen Eric, and Douglas Kellner. 1989. *Critical Theory and Society: A Reader*. London: Routledge.

Brunschwig, Henri. 1975. *Gesellschaft und Romantik in Preussen im 18. Jahrhundert*. Translated by Marie-Luise Schultheit. Frankfurt: Ullstein.

Carville, James, and Stan Greenberg. 2012. *It's the Middle Class, Stupid*. Washington, DC: Blue Rider.

Crèvecoeur, J. Hector St. John de. 1981 [1782]. *Letters from an American Farmer*. New York: Penguin Books.

Dalton, Russell. 2008. *The Good Citizen: How a Younger Generation Is Shaping American Politics*. Washington, DC: CQ Press.

Dewey, John. 1922. *Human Nature and Conduct*. New York: Random House Modern Library.

———. 1989 [1939]. *Freedom and Culture*. Amherst, MA: Prometheus Books.

Dillenberger, John, ed. 1961. *Martin Luther: Selections from His Writings*. New York: Doubleday Anchor.

Dobbs, Lew. 2006. *War on the Middle Class*. New York: Viking Penguin.

Du Bois, W. E. B. 2003 [1903]. *The Souls of Black Folk*. New York: Barnes and Noble Classics.

Durkheim, Emile. 1984 [1893]. *The Division of Labor in Society*. New York: Free Press.

———. 1951 [1897]. *Suicide*. New York: Free Press.

Elias, Norbert. 1989. *Studien über die Deutschen*. Edited by Michael Schröter. Frankfurt: Suhrkamp.

Etzioni, Amitai. 1997. *The New Golden Rule*. New York: Basic Books.

———, ed. 1998. *The Essential Communitarian Reader*. New York: Rowman and Littlefield.

Etzioni, Amitai, Andrew Volmert, and Elanit Rothschild. 2004. *The Communitarian Reader: Beyond the Essentials*. Lanham, MD: Rowman and Littlefield.

Faux, Jeff. 2012. *The Servant Economy*. New York: Wiley.

Friedson, Elliot. 1984. "The Changing Nature of Professional Control." *Annual Review of Sociology* 10: 1–20.

Habermas, Jürgen. 1962. *Strukturwandel der Öffentlichkeit.* Neuwied: Luchterhand.

Hacker, Jacob S., and Paul Pierson. 2010. *Winner Take All Politics.* New York: Simon and Schuster.

Hartz, Louis. 1991 [1955]. *The Liberal Tradition in America.* New York: Harvest Hill HBJ.

Hofstadter, Richard. 1955 [1944]. *Social Darwinism in American Thought.* Boston, MA: Beacon.

———. 1967. *The Paranoid Style in American Politics and Other Essays.* Boston, MA: Beacon.

Holborn, Hajo. 1981. *Deutsche Geschichte in der Neuzeit.* Frankfurt: Fischer Verlag.

Horkheimer, Max. 1972. *Critical Theory.* Translated by Matthew J. O'Connell. New York: Herder and Herder.

Jaspers, Karl. 1946. *Max Weber: Politiker, Forscher, Philosoph.* Bremen: Johs. Storm Verlag.

Jellinek, Georg. 1979 [1895]. *The Declaration of the Rights of Man and of Citizens.* Translated by Max Ferrand. Westport, CT: Hyperion.

Judt, Tony. 2011. *Thinking the Twentieth Century.* New York: New York University Press.

Kalberg, Stephen. 1980. "Max Weber's Types of Rationality: Cornerstones for the Analysis of Rationalization Processes in History." *American Journal of Sociology* 85(3): 1145–1179.

———. 1991. "The Hidden Link between Internal Political Culture and Cross-National Perceptions: Divergent Images of the Soviet Union in the United States and the FR of Germany." *Theory, Culture and Society* 8 (May): 31–56.

———. 1994. *Max Weber's Comparative-Historical Sociology.* Chicago, IL: University of Chicago Press.

———. 1997. "Tocqueville and Weber on the Sociological Origins of Citizenship: Political Culture of American Democracy." *Citizenship Studies* 1, 2 (July): 199–222.

———. 2003. "The Influence of Political Culture upon Cross-Cultural Misperceptions and Foreign Policy: United States and Germany." *German Politics and Society* 21, 3 (Fall): 1–24.

———. 2005. "Introduction: On 'Race' Membership, Common Ethnicity, the 'Ethnic Group,' and Heredity." Pp. 291–296 in *Max Weber: Readings and Commentary on Modernity*, edited by Stephen Kalberg. New York: Wiley-Blackwell.

————. 2011a. "Introduction to *The Protestant Ethic.*" Pp. 8–63 in Max Weber, *The Protestant Ethic and the Spirit of Capitalism.* Translated and introduced by Stephen Kalberg. New York: Oxford University Press.

————. 2011b. "Introduction to "the Protestant Sects." Pp. 183–208 in Max Weber, *The Protestant Ethic and the Spirit of Capitalism.* Translated and introduced by Stephen Kalberg. New York: Oxford University Press.

————. 2011c. "Max Weber." Pp. 305–373 in *The Wiley-Blackwell Companion to Major Social Theorists,* edited by George Ritzer and Jeffrey Stepnisky. Malden, MA: Wiley-Blackwell.

————. 2012. *Max Weber's Comparative-Historical Sociology Today: Major Themes, Modes of Analysis, and Applications.* Burlington, VT: Ashgate Publishers.

Keeter, Larry G. 1981. "Max Weber's Visit to North Carolina." *Journal of the History of Sociology* 3, 2 (Spring): 108–114.

Kellner, Douglas. 1989. *Critical Theory, Marxism and Modernity.* Baltimore, MD: Johns Hopkins University Press.

Klein, Naomi. 2007. *The Shock Doctrine.* New York: Henry Holt.

————. 2010. *No Logo: No Space, No Choice, No Jobs.* New York: Picador.

Kocka, Jürgen. 1981. *Die Angestellten in der deutschen Geschichte, 1850–1980.* Göttingen: Vandenhoeck and Ruprecht.

Kocka, Jürgen, and Gerhard Ritter, eds. 1974. *Deutsche Sozialgeschichte,* vol. 2. Munich: Verlag C. H. Beck.

Konwitz, Milton R., and Gail Kennedy. 1960. *The American Pragmatists.* Cleveland, OH: World Publishing Co.

Kotkin, Stephen. 2010. *Uncivil Society.* New York: Modern Library.

Lehmann, Hartmut, and Guenther Roth, eds. 1987. *Weber's Protestant Ethic: Origins, Evidence, Contexts.* Cambridge, UK: Cambridge University Press.

Lenger, Friedrich. 1994. *Werner Sombart 1863–1914: Eine Biographie.* Munich: Beck Verlag.

Lipset, Seymour Martin. 1979 [1963]. *The First New Nation.* New York: W. W. Norton.

Löwith, Karl. 1970 [1960]. "Weber's Interpretation of the Bourgeois-Capitalistic World in Terms of the Guiding Principle of 'Rationalization.'" Translated by Salvator Attanasio. Pp. 101–122 in *Max Weber,* edited by Dennis Wrong. Englewood Cliffs, NJ: Prentice-Hall.

Luce, Edward. 2012. *Time to Start Thinking.* New York: Atlantic Monthly Press.

Lynd, Robert S. 1967 [1939]. *Knowledge for What?* Princeton, NJ: Princeton University Press.

Lynd, Robert S., and Helen Merrell Lynd. 1956 [1929]. *Middletown.* New York: Harcourt Brace and World, Inc.

Manasse, Ernst Moritz. 1947. "Max Weber on Race." *Social Research* 14: 191–221.

Marcuse, Herbert. 1964. *One-Dimensional Man*. Boston, MA: Beacon Press.

Merton, Robert K. 1973. *The Sociology of Science*. Chicago, IL: University of Chicago Press.

Mommsen, Wolfgang. 1974. "Die Vereinigten Staaten von Amerika." Pp. 72–96 in *Max Weber: Gesellschaft, Politik und Geschichte*, edited by Wolfgang Mommsen. Frankfurt: Suhrkamp.

———. 1998. "Max Weber und die Vereinigten Staaten von Amerika." Pp. 91–103 in *Zwei Wege in die Moderne: Aspekte der deutsch-amerikanischen Beziehungen 1900–1918*, edited by Ragnhild Fiebig von Hase and Jürgen Heideking. Trier: Wissenschaftlicher Verlag.

———. 2000. "Max Weber in Amerika." *American Scholar* 69: 103–112.

Mosse, George. 1964. *The Crisis of German Ideology*. New York: Grosset and Dunlap.

Nelson, Benjamin. 1973. "Weber's Protestant Ethic: Its Origins, Wanderings, and Foreseeable Futures." Pp. 71–130 in *Beyond the Classics? Essays in the Scientific Study of Religion*, edited by Charles Y. Glock and Phillip E. Hammond. New York: Harper and Row.

Nussbaum, Martha. 2010. *Liberty of Conscience: In Defense of America's Tradition of Religious Equality*. New York: Basic Books.

Parsons, Talcott. 1966. *Societies: Evolutionary and Comparative Perspectives*. Englewood Cliffs, NJ: Prentice-Hall.

———. 1971. *The Evolution of Societies*. Edited and with an introduction by Jackson Toby. Englewood Cliffs, NJ: Prentice-Hall.

———. 2007. *American Society*. Edited and introduced by Giuseppe Sciortino. Boulder, CO: Paradigm.

Plessner, Helmut. 1974. *Die verspätete Nation*. Frankfurt: Suhrkamp.

Peukert, Detlev. 1989. *Max Webers Diagnose der Moderne*. Gottingen, Germany: Vandenhoeck & Ruprecht.

Putnam, Robert D. 2000. *Bowling Alone*. New York: Simon and Schuster.

Reich, Robert. 2008. *Super Capitalism: Transformation of Business, Democracy, and Everyday Life*. New York: Vintage.

———. 2011. *Aftershock: Next Economy and America's Future*. New York: Vintage.

———. 2012. *Beyond Outrage*. New York: Vintage.

Riesman, David. 1961 [1950]. *The Lonely Crowd*. New Haven, CT: Yale University Press.

Ringer, Fritz. 1969. *The Decline of the German Mandarins*. Cambridge: Harvard University Press.

Rollman, Hans. 1993. "'Meet Me in St. Louis': Troeltsch and Weber in America." Pp. 357–384 in *Weber's Protestant Ethic*, edited by Hartmut Lehmann and Guenther Roth. New York: Cambridge University Press.

Roth, Guenther. 1985. "Marx and Weber in the United States—Today." Pp. 215–233 in *A Marx-Weber Dialogue*, edited by Robert J. Antonio and Ronald M. Glassman. Lawrence: University Press of Kansas.

———. 1987. *Politische Herrschaft und persönliche Freiheit*. Frankfurt: Suhrkamp.

———. 1997. "The Young Max Weber: Anglo-American Religious Influences and Protestant Social Reform in Germany." *International Journal of Politics, Culture and Society* 10: 659–671.

———. 2001. *Max Webers deutsch-englische Familiengeschichte, 1800–1950*. Tuebingen: Mohr Siebeck.

———. 2005a. "Europäisierung, Amerikanisierung und Yankeetum. Zum New Yorker Besuch von Max und Marianne Weber 1904." Pp. 9–32 in *Asketischer Protestantismus und der "Geist" des modernen Kapitalismus*, edited by Wolfgang Schluchter and Friedrich Wilhelm Graf. Tübingen: Mohr Siebeck.

———. 2005b. "Transatlantic Connections: A Cosmopolitan Context for Max and Marianne Weber's New York Visit 1904." *Max Weber Studies* 5, 1 (January): 81–112.

Rueschemeyer, Dietrich. 1973. *Lawyers and Their Society*. Cambridge, MA: Harvard University Press.

Savelsberg, Joachim. 1994. "Knowledge, Domination and Criminal Punishment." *American Journal of Sociology* 99, 4: 911–943.

———. 1999. "Knowledge, Domination, and Criminal Punishment Revisited: Incorporating State Socialism." *Punishment and Society* 1, 1: 45–70.

Savelsberg, Joachim, and Ryan D. King. 2005. "Institutionalizing Collective Memories of Hate: Law and Law Enforcement in Germany and the United States." *American Journal of Sociology* 111, 2: 579–616.

Scaff, Lawrence. 1998. "The 'Cool Objectivity of Sociation': Max Weber and Marianne Weber in America." *History of the Human Sciences* 11, 2: 61–82.

———. 2005. "Remnants of Romanticism: Max Weber in Oklahoma and Indian Territory." Pp. 77–110 in *The Protestant Ethic Turns 100*, edited by William H. Swatos and Lutz Kaelber. Boulder, CO: Paradigm

———. 2011. *Max Weber in America*. Princeton, NJ: Princeton University Press.

Schudson, Michael. 1998. *The Good Citizen: A History of American Civic Life*. New York: Free Press.

Selznick, Phillip. 1992. *The Moral Commonwealth*. Berkeley: University of California Press.

————. 2004. *Leadership in Administration: A Sociological Interpretation.* Berkeley: University of California Press.

Smith, Adam. 1981 [1776]. *An Inquiry into the Nature and Causes of the Wealth of Nations*, vols. I and II. Edited by R. H. Campbell and A. S. Skinner. Indianapolis, IN: Liberty Fund.

Stern, Fritz. 1965. *The Politics of Cultural Despair.* New York: Anchor Books.

Stiglitz, Joseph E. 2012. *The Price of Inequality.* New York: Norton.

Sullivan, William M. 1995. *Work and Integrity.* New York: Harper Business.

Sumner, Graham. 1906. *Volkways.* Boston, MA: Ginn.

Tocqueville, Alexis de. 1945 [1835]. *Democracy in America* (2 vols.). New York: Vintage.

Toennies, Ferdinand. 1957 [1887]. *Community and Society.* Translated by Charles P. Loomis. New York: Harper Torchbooks.

Troeltsch, Ernst. 1960 [1911]. *The Social Teachings of the Christian Churches* (2 vols.). New York: Harper Torchbooks.

Veblen, Thorstein. 1953 [1899]. *The Theory of the Leisure Class.* New York: Mentor Books.

Weber, Marianne. 1975 [1926]. *Max Weber.* Translated by Harry Zohn. New York: Wiley and Sons.

Weber, Max. 1927 [1923]. *General Economic History.* Translated by Frank H. Knight. Glencoe, IL: Free Press.

————. 1930. *The Protestant Ethic and the Spirit of Capitalism.* Translated by Talcott Parsons. London: Allen Unwin.

————. 1936. *Jugendbriefe.* Edited by Marianne Weber. Tübingen: Mohr Siebeck

————. 1946a. "Capitalism and Rural Society in Germany." Pp. 363–385 in *From Max Weber*, edited and translated by H. H. Gerth and C. Wright Mills. New York: Oxford.

————. 1946b [1919]. "Politics as a Vocation." Pp. 77–128 in *From Max Weber*, edited and translated by H. H. Gerth and C. Wright Mills. New York: Oxford.

————. 1946c [1920]. "Religious Rejections of the World." Pp. 323–359 in *From Max Weber*, edited and translated by H. H. Gerth and C. Wright Mills. New York: Oxford.

————. 1946d [1917/1919]. "Science as a Vocation." Pp. 129–156 in *From Max Weber*, edited and translated by H. H. Gerth and C. Wright Mills. New York: Oxford.

————. 1946e [1920]. "The Social Psychology of the World Religions." Pp. 267–301 in *From Max Weber*, edited and translated by H. H. Gerth and C. Wright Mills. New York: Oxford.

————. 1949 [1922]. *The Methodology of the Social Sciences.* Edited and translated by Edward A. Shils and Henry A. Finch. New York: Free Press.

————. 1968 [1921]. *Economy and Society*. Edited by Guenther Roth and Claus Wittich and translated by Roth, Wittich, et al. Berkeley: University of California Press.

————. 1971a [1910]. "Max Weber on Race and Society." Introduction by Benjamin Nelson and translated by Jerome Gittleman. *Social Research* 38, 1 (Spring): 30–41.

————. 1971b [1924]. "Socialism." Pp. 191–219 in *Max Weber*, edited by J. E. T. Eldridge. London: Nelson and Sons.

————. 1972 [1910]. "Antikritisches zum 'Geist' des Kapitalismus." Pp. 149–187 in *Max Weber: Die protestantische Ethik II, Kritiken und Antikritiken*, edited by Johannes Winckelmann. Hamburg: Siebenstern Verlag.

————. 1973 [1910]. "Max Weber, Dr. Alfred Ploetz, and W. E. B. Du Bois." Edited and translated by Benjamin Nelson and Jerome Gittleman. *Sociological Analysis* 34(4): 308–312.

————. 1976 [1909]. *The Agrarian Sociology of Ancient Civilizations*. Translated by R. I. Frank. London: New Left Books.

————. 1978 [1906]. "The Prospects for Liberal Democracy in Tsarist Russia." Pp. 269–284 in *Weber: Selections in Translation*, edited by W. G. Runciman. Cambridge: Cambridge University Press.

————. 1985 [1906]. "'Churches' and 'Sects' in North America: An Ecclesiastical Socio-Political Sketch." Translated by Colin Loader. *Sociological Theory* 3: 7–13.

————. 1988 [1924]. "Geschäftsbericht und Diskussionsreden auf den Deutschen soziologischen Tagungen (1910, 1912)." Pp. 431–491 in *Gesammelte Aufsätze zur Soziologie und Sozialpolitik*, edited by Marianne Weber. Tübingen: Mohr Siebeck.

————. 1994 [1917]. "Suffrage and Democracy in Germany." Pp. 80–129 in *Weber: Political Writings*, edited by Peter Lassman and Ronal Speirs and translated by Ronald Speirs. New York: Cambridge.

————. 1996 [1906]. "Zur Lage der bürgerlichen Demokratie in Rußland." Pp. 1–104 in Zur Russischen Revolution von 1905: Schriften und Reden 1905–1912 (Max Weber Gesamtausgabe I/10 Studienausgabe). Edited by Wolfgang J. Mommsen. Tübingen: Mohr Siebeck.

————. 2001 [1907–1910]. *The Protestant Ethic Debate: Max Weber's Replies to His Critics, 1907–1910*. Edited by David Chalcraft and Austin Harrington and translated by Harrington and Mary Shields. Liverpool: Liverpool University Press.

————. 2002 [1920]. *The Protestant Ethic and the Spirit of Capitalism*. Translated and introduced by Stephen Kalberg. Los Angeles, CA: Roxbury Publishing.

————. 2005. *Max Weber: Readings and Commentary on Modernity*. Edited by Stephen Kalberg. New York: Wiley-Blackwell Publishers.

————. 2009. *The Protestant Ethic and the Spirit of Capitalism with Other Writings on the Rise of the West.* Translated and introduced by Stephen Kalberg. New York: Oxford.

————. 2011a [1906]. "'Churches' and 'Sects' in North America: An Ecclesiastical Sociopolitical Sketch." Translated by Colin Loader; revised by Stephen Kalberg. Pp. 227–232 in Max Weber, *The Protestant Ethic and the Spirit of Capitalism.* Translated and introduced by Stephen Kalberg. New York: Oxford.

————. 2011b [1910]. "A Final Rebuttal to a Critic of "Spirit of Capitalism." Pp. 256–271 in *The Protestant Ethic and the Spirit of Capitalism.* Translated and introduced by Stephen Kalberg. New York: Oxford.

————. 2011c [1920]. *The Protestant Ethic and the Spirit of Capitalism.* Translated and introduced by Stephen Kalberg. New York: Oxford.

————. 2011d [1920]. "The Protestant Sects and the Spirit of Capitalism." Pp. 209–226 in *The Protestant Ethic and the Spirit of Capitalism.* Translated and introduced by Stephen Kalberg. New York: Oxford.

White, Morton. 1957 [1947]. *Social Thought in America.* Boston, MA: Beacon Press.

Winter, Elke. 2004. *Max Weber et les rélations ethniques. Du refus du biologisme racial á l'État multinational.* Quebec: Presses de l'Université Laval.

Wolin, Sheldon. 2008. *Democracy Incorporated.* Princeton, NJ: Princeton University Press.

Credits

The author gratefully acknowledges permission granted by several publishers to reprint in this volume sections of previously published chapters and articles.

Oxford University Press. For republication of extracts from pp. 39–43 of Introduction to Part 1 and from pp. 183–189, 191–197, and 220–225 of Introduction to Part 2 of Max Weber, *The Protestant Ethic and the Spirit of Capitalism*, translated and introduced by Stephen Kalberg. New York, 2011. By permission of Oxford University Press, USA.

Sage Publications. For republication of extracts from pp. 127–133 of "Max Weber's Analysis of the Unique American Civic Sphere." *Journal of Classical Sociology* 9, 1 (February 2009) (http://online.sagepub.com).

Sheffield Academic Press. For republication of extracts from pp. 179–185 of "The Modern World as a Monolithic Iron Cage? Utilizing Max Weber to Define the Internal Dynamics of American Political Culture Today." *Max Weber Studies* 1, 2 (May 2001).

Index

"Achievement society," 96n6
Activism: associations-based, 92–93;
   religious origins of, 26–31
Activity-oriented individualism, 62
Addams, Jane, 119
American Civil Liberties Union, 66n5
Arab Spring, 110–111
Associations: business, 48; origins
   of in religion, 35–36, 51–54;
   professional associations model,
   88–91, 94–95; Weber on, 35–36,
   48. *See also* Civic associations
Authority: hostility to, by sect,
   43; Puritan views of, 66n3

Baxter, Richard, 43, 128, 129
Belief: Puritans as acting in reference
   to, 24–26; religious faith and, 23
Bellah, Robert, 116n12
"Benevolent feudalism," 57n8
Bentham, Jeremy, 61
Boston, Weber in, 122–123
Bourgeoisie, birth and growth of, 62
Bureaucratic organization, Weber
   on, 71–72, 77–78, 95
Bush, George W., 87

Calvin, John, 27, 128
Capitalism: coercive aspects of,
   76–77; critical theory and,
   115n8; on frontier, 120–121;

German views of US, 123; in
   Germany, 63–64, 65; mechanical
   foundations of, 70–72, 132–134;
   power of material goods, 78–81;
   Puritan embrace of, 62, 129–130.
   See also Spirit of capitalism
Chicago, Weber on, 119–120
Church, sect compared to, 37–39
Civic associations: activism of, 92–93;
   decline of, 89; development and
   transformation of, 13–14; in
   Germany, 65; membership in, 52;
   pluralism of, 98n15; practical-
   ethical action of, 54–56; social
   honor and, 51; Tocqueville and,
   3, 35, 56n5, 114n2, 114n5
Civic ideals, 52, 54–56, 93
Civic individualism: development
   of, 55, 60; dissolution of civic
   sphere and, 80; features of, 62; in
   generalization model, 84–85; in
   nineteenth century, 103–106. *See
   also* Practical-ethical individualism
Civic sphere: challenges to, 68–69,
   70; colonization of, 4; contraction
   of, 3; development of, 13, 26, 28;
   dissolution of, 75–81, 116n14;
   ethical community of Puritans
   and, 29–30; fundamental beliefs
   for, 21–22; generalization model
   and, 84–88; group formation and,

49; importance of, 9; origins and
features of, 51–54; professional
associations and, 90–91;
salience of, 54. *See also* Spirit of
democracy; Symbiotic dualism
Classical Liberalism, 61
"Common man," characteristics
of, 61–62
Common values of civic sphere, 9
Communitarian literature, 18n3–4
Communitarian school, 57n12
Community activism, religious
origins of, 26–31
Community life, loss of, 3
Community service, 31n6, 94
Conflict model, 91–95
Conformity among faithful, 23, 37
Consumerist ethos, 79–80
Corruption, Weber view of, 69, 126n22
Crisis commentary: critique of,
6, 7–8, 58n16, 100, 101;
overview of, 3–4, 5, 99–100

Democracy: in Africa and Middle
East, 110–111; participatory, in
sect, 43; plebiscitary, 126n23;
routes to, 107, 109–110. *See
also* Spirit of democracy
Du Bois, W. E. B., 120
Dualism: individualism-consumer,
79–80; in Puritan values, 28, 102–
103. *See also* Symbiotic dualism
Durkheim, Emile, 3, 117n14
Dynamism of American culture, 92–93

Economy and Society (Weber),
83, 117n19
Economy of Germany, 63–64
England, democracy in, 107
Ethical action, orientation
toward, 131–132
Ethical community: development
of, 28–31; professional
association as, 88–91; of
Puritan sect, 37, 39, 40, 41

Ethos, 24
Europeanization model, 77–78, 123
Evil, mastering of, by Puritans, 29–30
Evolutionary axioms, Weber
on, 107, 109–110
Expulsion from sect, 40

France, democracy in, 107
Franklin, Benjamin, 48, 131
Frontier, Weber on, 120–121

Generalization model, 84–88, 94–95
German Romanticism, 116n13
Germany: view of state in,
63–66, 73–74; view of
US capitalism in, 123
Gore, Al, 96n6
Group formation: business
groups, 48; eminent power
of ascetic Protestantism and,
49–51; as swift and nimble,
30, 35; Weber on, 30, 34

Hold-your-own individualism,
40, 41, 52
Horatio Alger model, 61, 62, 68–69
Hostility to authority by sect, 43

Individual, view of in
industrializing US, 61–62
Individualism: activity-oriented, 62;
cultivation of, 81; hold-your-own,
40, 41, 52; practical-ethical, 13, 14,
84–85, 114n4; practical-rational,
114n4; Tocqueville view of, 113n1,
115n11; Weber on, 25, 103–106,
113n1; world-mastery, 13, 22–26,
30. *See also* Civic individualism
Individualism-consumer
dualism, 79–80
Industrialization in Germany and
view of state, 63–66, 73–74
Industrialization in US: view
of state and, 60–63, 74;
Weber view of, 70–73

Integrating values, 42
"Iron cage" metaphor for modern
    era, 14, 15, 69–75, 133

Kelley, Florence, 119
Kennedy, John F., 2
Kerry, John, 87–88

Laws, Weber on, 107–109
Luther, Martin, 46n15
Lutheranism in Germany, 64, 65

Macrostructural transformations
    and political culture, 11
Marx, Karl, 116n13
Material goods, power of, 78–81
Membership: in civic associations,
    52; in sects, 38, 39, 40
Merton, Robert K., 97n9
Methodical-rational organization
    of life, 42, 129–131
Middle class, diminution of, 3–4
Mill, John Stuart, 61
Mode of analysis of Weber, 7,
    10–12, 100–101, 106–112
Moral campaigns, 93
Moral values in 2004 presidential
    election, 85–88

New crisis analysis. See
    Crisis commentary
New Gilded Age, 4, 99–100
New Orleans, Weber in, 121
New York, Weber and, 118–119
Nietzsche, Friedrich, 73, 116n13
North Carolina, Weber in, 122

Obama, Barack, 1
Oklahoma, Weber on, 120–121

Paine, Thomas, 66n5
Parsonian theorizing, 96n3, 115n8
Participatory democracy in sect, 43
Past, embedding of present in, 11
Plebiscitary democracy, 126n23

Pluralism of civic associations, 98n15
"Policing" tasks of state, 57n12
Political culture: central contours and
    long-range pathways of, 12–14;
    complementary construct for,
    83–84; components of, 30–31, 112;
    dynamism of, 55; group-formation
    capacities and, 51; historical
    dimensions of, 6–8, 100–101,
    102–106; of late nineteenth and
    early twentieth centuries, 59–66;
    longevity of, 106–109; mode of
    analysis, 10–12; questions regarding,
    9–10; religion and, 12–14, 34; spirit
    of democracy and, 5–6; study of,
    109–112; themes of, 66; uniqueness
    of US, 65, 73–74; Weber on, 7,
    34, 55–56; Weberian model of, 70,
    75–81, 83, 95. See also Civic sphere
Political culture approach,
    overview of, 8–10
Political fragmentation, 2–3
Populism, 57n7
Power: distribution of, 3–4; of
    material goods, 78–81
Practical-ethical action: of associations,
    54–56, 60; in conflict model,
    91–95; in German society, 64–65
Practical-ethical individualism, 13,
    14, 84–85, 114n4. See also Civic
    individualism; Symbiotic dualism;
    World-mastery individualism
Practical-rational individualism, 114n4
Practical rationalism, expansion of,
    70, 71–72, 75–77, 80–81
Predestination, doctrine of, 36, 128
Presidential campaigns: of 2004,
    85–88; of 2012, 1, 2
Prestige of membership in sects, 40
Priests and trust, 37–38
Privatization of work, 75–77
Professional associations
    model, 88–91, 94–95
Protestant ethic: development of,
    24–25, 128–130; evolution of, to

spirit of capitalism, 130–132; loss of religious foundation of, 47–48

The Protestant Ethic and the Spirit of Capitalism (Weber): evolution of, 130–132; mechanical foundations, 132–133; on methodology, 117n17; on orientation toward work, 70; overview of, 36, 127, 134; publication of, 33; spiritual foundation, 128–130

Protestantism, ascetic. *See* Puritan values

Public service, expectations for, 2

Puritan values: community orientation, 26–28; dualism in, 28, 102–103; ethical conduct, 28–31, 37, 39, 40, 41; influence of, 51, 59–60; integrating values, 42; in presidential campaign of 2004, 86–88; rights of individuals, 44; social carriers of, 13–14, 131–132; style of life, 129; work ethic, 128–129; world-mastery individualism and, 22–26. *See also* Capitalism

Putnam, Robert, 3, 99

Race relations, Weber on, 121–122

Religion: conformity and, 23, 37; in Germany, 64, 65; origins of associations in, 35–36, 51–54; origins of community activism in, 26–31; origins of world-mastery individualism in, 22–26; political culture and, 12–14, 34; Protestant ethic and, 47–48, 128–130. *See also* Puritan values; Salvation ethos of Puritans

Romney, Mitt, 1

Salvation ethos of Puritans: ethical purity and, 38–39; group formation and, 49–50; Predestination doctrine and, 129; testifying to salvation status, 36–37; world-mastery individualism and, 23–24, 25–26

Sandpile atomization: group formation compared to, 34, 35, 48, 49–51, 69, 103; view of US society as, 15

Science, ethos of, 97n9

Sect: church compared to, 37–39; self-governance of, 43; service orientation of, 41, 49; social-psychological dynamic of, 39–42

"Sects" (Weber), 33–34, 37

Self-governance of sect, 39–40, 43

Self-reliance–shared community spectrum, 1–2, 8

Service orientation of sect, 41, 49

Simmel, Georg, 73

Smith, Adam, 61

Social Darwinism, 62

Social honor: civic associations and, 36, 51; salience of, 40–41

Social milieu, 52

Social-psychological dynamic of sect, 39–42

Social sciences, Weber on, 107–109

"Sociation" mode, 50

Spirit of capitalism, 48, 70, 130–132. *See also The Protestant Ethic and the Spirit of Capitalism* (Weber)

Spirit of democracy: components of, 1–2, 4–5, 13–14; longevity of, 106–109; multiple "exclusivities" as characterizing, 48–49; poles of, 4, 55; political culture and, 5–6

St. Louis Universal Exposition and Congress of Arts and Science, 118, 120

State: "policing" tasks of, 57n12; view of in industrializing Germany, 63–66, 73–74; view of in industrializing US, 60–63

"Steel-hard casing" metaphor, 15. *See also* "Iron cage" metaphor for modern era

Stockyards of Chicago, Weber on, 120

Strong individual–small state constellation, 59–66

Subjective meaningfulness, 23–24

Symbiotic dualism: described, 13, 55; importance of, 112; as uniquely American, 31; weakening of, 79, 80; Weber on, 102–103. *See also* Civic sphere; Practical-ethical individualism

Tocqueville, Alexis de: civic associations and, 3, 35, 56n5, 114n2, 114n5; civic sphere and, 117n14; fear of egalitarianism of, 58n15; individualism and, 113n1, 115n11; master-key concept of, 31
Traditional economic ethic, 128–129, 130
Troeltsch, Ernst, 119
Tuskegee Institute, Weber visit to, 122

Utilitarianism, 61

Values: civic associations and, 52–54; compromise and, 114n4; moral, in 2004 election, 85–88; religious, and development of political culture, 12–14; worldviews and, 91–92. *See also* Civic ideals; Puritan values
Vocational calling, 70, 77, 128, 131
Volunteerism, 2

Wealth: distribution of, 3–4; as evidence of God's favor, 27, 129–130; as praise of God's majesty, 24; search for, 128
Weber, Marianne, 118, 119, 120
Weber, Max: on associations, 35–36, 48; on belief, 23; on "benevolent feudalism," 57n8; on bureaucratic organization, 71–72, 77–78, 95; on capitalism, 70–71; on civic

associations, 52–53, 54; on civic sphere, 68–69; on corruption, 69, 126n22; on development of civic sphere, 26; *Economy and Society*, 83, 117n19; on ethical conduct, 29; on frontier, 120–121; on group formation, 30, 34, 49–51; on individualism, 25, 103–106, 113n1; on industrialization, 70–73; "iron cage" metaphor of, 14, 15, 69–75, 133; mode of analysis, 7, 10–12, 100–101, 106–112; on political culture, 7, 34, 55–56; on Protestant ethic, 47–48; on Protestant sects, 33–34; on Puritan conduct, 28; on Puritan sects, 39–42; on race relations, 121–122; on religion and culture, 12–14, 31; on salvation ethos of Puritans, 38–39; on sect compared to church, 37–39; "Sects," 33–34, 37; on self-governance of sect, 43; on social sciences, 107–109; on symbiotic dualism, 102–103; visit to US by, 118–124; on worldviews, 91. *See also The Protestant Ethic and the Spirit of Capitalism* (Weber)
Weberian analysis, 84
Weberian model of political culture, 70, 75–81, 83, 95
Winthrop, John, 1
Work: intensification and elevation of, 27, 128–129; methodical orientation toward, 70–72; privatization of, 75–77. *See also* Vocational calling
World-mastery individualism, 13, 22–26, 30
Worldviews, 91–92

About the Author

Stephen Kalberg, Associate Professor of Sociology at Boston University, teaches courses on American society, classical theory, contemporary theory, and comparative political cultures. He is the author of *Max Weber's Comparative-Historical Sociology* (University of Chicago Press 1994) and *Max Weber's Comparative-Historical Sociology Today* (Ashgate 2012), the translator and editor of *Max Weber: The Protestant Ethic and the Spirit of Capitalism with Other Writings on the Rise of the West* (Oxford 2009), the translator of *Max Weber: The Protestant Ethic and the Spirit of Capitalism* (Oxford 2011), and the editor of *Max Weber: Readings and Commentary on Modernity* (Wiley-Blackwell 2005). His general introduction to Weber's works, published in *The Wiley-Blackwell Companion to Major Social Theorists* (2003, 2011), has appeared in book form in German, Spanish, Portuguese, Turkish, and Italian. He has also published on the political and economic cultures of Germany and the United States.

"In this gem of a book Stephen Kalberg relies on Max Weber to unravel the historical roots of American political culture. The spirit of American democracy has been marked by a pendulum swinging between the poles of self-reliance and civic engagement. This concise and weighty book offers insight and illumination as we ponder whether polarization is all that is left when the pendulum stops moving."

—Peter Katzenstein, Cornell University

"Stephen Kalberg has developed a beautifully relevant Weberian analysis of the conflicted trajectory of contemporary American society. He accomplishes this with a concise text that nevertheless leaves nothing out, except the tedium of scholasticism. Kalberg is especially luminous in his treatment of the translation of ethical individualism into a secular creed sustained by the densely populated world of politically interested civic organizations, his exploration of the ways this morally animated civil society has been a force against the iron cage of an increasingly bureaucratized political economy, and his sensitive analysis of why the reproduction of this civilizing force is fragile and problematic in the twenty-first century."

—Michael Schwartz, Stony Brook University

The ongoing debate over the "crisis of American democracy" is a topic replete with speculation. Using Weber's long-term perspective, the book provides rich new insights—and some reasons for optimism. It also offers powerful explanations for the particular contours of today's American political culture.

Kalberg draws upon Weber to reconstruct political culture in ways that define America's unique spirit of democracy. Developing several Weber-inspired models, Kalberg reveals patterns of oscillation in American history. Can these pendulum movements sustain today the symbiotic dualism that earlier invigorated American democracy? Can they do so to such an extent that the American spirit of democracy is rejuvenated? Balanced in approach, the book questions the prevailing perspective that American democracy is mostly in decline.